FROM GRANDPA WITH LOVE

The Adventures, Stories and Yarns of a Lifelong Fisherman and Hunter

By

T.D. Roth

ISBN: 978-1-9991125-4-7

Cover Image by Kris from Pixaby

Dedicated

To

Toby, Tyler, Keegan
and Colton

Read this First!

This is a collection of adventures, stories, and yarns accumulated over a lifetime of fishing and hunting. Of necessity I've changed a few names. Due to faulty memory some towns and lakes have been given fictitious names from Greek words with meanings such as "nowhere" or "lost" or other foolishness. Occasionally separate stories are blended together, and tall tales have been written in the first person. Truth and fiction are highly embellished throughout, so let the reader beware.

TABLE OF CONTENTS

My Side of the Mountain ____ 1
Wild Turkey ____ 16
Daffy Ducks ____ 31
The Crawdad Hole ____ 38
White Tails ____ 46
City Slickers ____ 55
Alligators of the North ____ 66
Beating the Bush ____ 78
It Only Takes One ____ 83
Journey to The Wind-Swept Land ____ 101
Troutin' ____ 108
Skipper Tom ____ 123
Dusty and the Bear ____ 133
Ole the Swede ____ 164
Make Up Your Mind ____ 169
Chelsea ____ 177
Wild Boars ____ 194
The Bass Master ____ 203
Ice Jiggers ____ 215
O'Hair Air ____ 225

MY SIDE OF THE MOUNTAIN

MY SIDE OF the Mountain by Jean Craighead George was my favorite book as a boy. Living off the land; knowing the wild plants; setting snares for rabbits; and catching fish by whatever means intrigued me. Sam Gribley, the main character in the book, was my hero. Many a time I substituted the J in *WWJD (What Would Jesus Do?)* to *WWSD (What Would Sam Do?)* I like Jesus and he certainly knows where the fish are, but Sam was more into the things boys do.

Having parents who grew up in the Dirty Thirties left its mark on me. "Poaching" was something rich folks did with eggs and had nothing to do with shooting a deer or catching a fish out of season. There were only three basic game laws. First, did you need the meat?

Second, don't shoot what you won't eat. Third, don't get caught by a game warden. What officers thought to be legal and what we believed to be moral were different. After all, the Lord helps those who help themselves.

My first exposure to guns was from my Grandpa Allen. Most of the cousins remember him as a grumpy old geezer and downright scary. What other grandpa would loosen his false teeth and shake them between his lips like a skull in a horror movie? If you let the screen door slam as you made your escape, he'd holler and threaten to get you. For some reason he thought that was really funny. Grandpa smoked cigarettes and pipes and he chewed tobacco and snorted snuff. The paint was peeling from the side of his car from the juice he spat out the window.

I might have been his favorite grandchild if it hadn't been for the ashtray incident. Grandpa loved his afternoon nap. He'd place his false teeth on a side table, lounge back on his recliner, and snore away. His mouth was wide open. He snorted on the inhale and flapped his loose lips on the exhale. Drops of pale brown spittle ran from the corners of his mouth. As a four-year-old I found that the most fascinating thing I had ever seen. As he breathed in, I'd step forward to look at this wobbly thing in the back of his throat that reminded me of a little punching bag. Then I'd step back as his terrible smelling breath was expelled. During this process I noticed that his ashtray was overflowing with old cigarette butts. It seemed like the most natural thing in the world to pick up the ashtray and pour it down that cavernous throat on the next intake. You better believe that the screen door slammed that day. If Grandpa hadn't been brought to his knees hacking, hawking, and wheezing for breath, I probably wouldn't be writing this. I was sent home and not welcomed back for a long time.

Now, to Grandpa's gun. He had an air pistol that could shoot bbs or pellets. The actual barrel holding the bbs was only two inches long, so you can guess the accuracy. Grandpa would sit on his back steps watching for neighborhood cats to appear. *Blam!* He got the biggest kick out of peppering feline behinds. No cats were leaving calling cards in the dirt around his plants. His greatest enjoyment came from shooting at stray dogs, especially the males. He'd let a mutt sniff around, waiting until it lifted a leg. *Pow!* Right in the "you know where." There's no way to describe the painful yelp and speedy skedaddle of a pooch in pain. A little boy can learn a lot from his grandpa.

I was seven years old when we moved to a twenty-acre farm in Payette, Idaho. It was a great place to grow up. My friends and I explored the foothills, dug caves, and threw dirt clods. I collected just about everything a young boy can find: arrowheads, rocks, bones, shed snake skins. You might say I was hunting long before I had a rifle.

Southern Idaho was renowned for pheasant hunting in the 1950s. Coveys of quail fed in our wheat field. Thousands of ducks landed in the stubble behind our house every fall. Mourning doves came and went with the seasons. Further north were mule and whitetail deer. Idaho also has moose, elk, bear, bighorn sheep, mountain goats, cougars, and wolves. If you have the means, it's a hunter's paradise. We were among those that lacked the means.

Dinah, our little black spaniel, was a born hunter. She roamed the fields from dawn to dusk. If our neighbor, Henry Sailor, hadn't shot her through a front leg, she would have made a wonderful hunting dog. After limping around the farm for several weeks in a cast, she wanted nothing to do with guns. She was so gun-shy that if I picked up a long stick, she hid under the house. Incidentally, our house didn't have a foundation, just some well-placed cinderblocks that supported the floor beams. A door in the floor of the back porch lifted where narrow wooden steps descended into a dirt-walled cellar. My mom kept her preserves there. My favorite was home-canned pears. Some had a drop or two of red food coloring and some a drop or two of green. They were so good! The cellar was infested with mice. Black widow spiders peered from their funneled webs in the corners of the shelves. I never liked going down there. I'd grab a couple jars of canned fruit and run! Dinah didn't seem to mind the mice or spiders that lived under her part the house.

Our cat, Tom, what an original name, was a fantastic hunter. He once leapt three feet into the air to bring down a pheasant as it lifted in flight. Tom hobbled around the yard with casts on both front legs for a time. Henry Sailor had half a dozen pussycats and couldn't tolerate tomcats. He should have fixed those tabbies because he was a bad shot. Two broken legs didn't dissuade Tom from doing his thing. You can't keep a good tomcat down.

Dad introduced me to fishing with a willow branch and eight feet of line. My first fish was a big fat carp. You might say that I hooked the fish and fishing hooked me. I was bound and determined to get a rod and reel. My folks weren't the type to give you things. I had to buy my own. The Merc, a small department store in Payette, had a beautiful Zebco reel in the display case. Only $6.99 stood between me and my fishing dream, a lot of money in the 1950s. I paid down a dollar on a lay-way program. Only $5.99 to go.

My weekly allowance of fifty cents was just enough to get into a movie, buy a five cent Sugar Daddy, and have a dime for the 5 and 10 Cent Store. Ten cents would buy a pea shooter and a small bag of peas. My best friend and I enjoyed peppering the teenagers who swam in the local canal and then escaping on our bicycles. Sacrifices would have to be made to buy that reel. I rode my bicycle along the back roads collecting pop and beer bottles. There was a two-cent refund for a pop bottle and one cent for a beer bottle. When strawberry season came, I dutifully boarded the back of a truck every morning. A good morning of strawberry picking netted another fifty cents. Every week I went to the Merc with twenty-five or fifty cents. The lady drew a small card from her file, marked my payment, and showed me the balance. My dad mercifully paid the last two dollars. It was time to go fishing!

My Uncle Bill was only two years older than me and more like a cousin than an uncle. He had a big male spaniel named Red. We'd take our bikes, fishing poles, and dogs to the Payette River. Entire days were spent exploring. Our favorite spot was behind Wells and

Davies, an abattoir overlooking the river. Blood from the slaughterhouse rippled and spiraled into the clear river water in rich pink and purple whirls. It was a wonder to behold. The biggest suckers and carp imaginable swam to that spot to feed on scraps of fat and offal. They were not fish you take home, but we loved catching them. Most were thrown into the brush. Dinah and Red spent the day nosing up and down the bank and rolling in one dead sucker after another – doggy perfume. And the smell... I had to scrub Dinah after every trip. Even then, as soon as she got wet, back came that indescribable yet unmistakable smell of rotten fish.

We sometimes fished on the Snake River. A few channel catfish lurked around the pylons of the bridges. We were just catching the babies. Bill convinced me that their whiskers were poisonous, that they would sting you if you touched them. It's challenging getting one of those little devils off a hook without touching its whiskers. I usually cut the line and tied on a new hook. Can you imagine how hard it is to clean a fish without touching its head? I learned to nail the head to a board and then peel the skin off the body with a pair of pliers. Great eating!

My Grandma Wanda warned us, "Don't you ever go swimming in the Snake River. It's broad and fast and full of undertows. Every year some little boy gets sucked under and drowns. If I ever catch you, you'll get the tanning of your life!" Well... There was this one time that we spotted a large burlap bag floating in the middle of the river. It was the oddest thing. Reminded me of a big balloon. Even odder, it was stuck in the current with the water forming a wake around it.

"Bill!" Look at that bag," I said. "Why isn't it floating down the river?"

Bill shielded his eyes from the sun and frowned. "I'll bet there are baby kittens in that bag. That's how people kill the cats they don't want."

"What if they're not dead?" I asked. "We might be able to save them."

Bill held his chin between a thumb and forefinger, then pursed his lips with a wise look he had learned from my Uncle Lee. "I've got a plan," he said. "We'll tie the ends of a rope around our wastes. If I get pulled off my feet by an undertow, you can pull me back. If you get pulled down, I'll hold you."

We stripped down to our shorts and waded into the water. Bill carried a long pole which he used to probe the bottom for holes. The muddy water came up to our knees, then to our wastes, and finally just below our armpits. So far. So good. Slowly, slowly we edged to the middle of the river. I braced myself in the current, steadying Bill as he pulled on the bag. It was attached to about twelve feet of rope and anchored to the bottom with a large rock. He untied the neck of the sack and shook the bag into the water. A bloated cow stomach fell out and bobbed down the river, followed by a large intestine and about a mile of small intestine and guts. We were impressed. Never figured out why someone would go to all that trouble.

"What in tarnation are you boys doing in the middle of the river?" It was Grandma. She'd had a premonition that we were up to something and come looking for us.

We didn't get a whipping, but we didn't fish on the Snake River for a long time after that.

I got my second dog on one of our forays along the Payette River. An old timer pulled up in a rusty Chevy pickup. "Ya wouldn't like a little puppy, would ya?" he asked.

I looked at a cute little ball of black fur. "How big does it get? My mom's been wanting a little dog to keep her company."

"Not big at all. This would be the perfect dog for your ma."

That "perfect" dog grew up to be a Labrador retriever, not exactly the little lap dog Mom had in mind. We named her Lady. She would have made a great duck dog if she hadn't been hit by a car. Death is a fact of life on the farm. Calves were raised to be eaten. Old hens met their Maker at the chopping block. A headless chicken is a wonder to behold.

GRANDMA WAS fifty percent Ute. Her mother, Great Grandma Baker, had homesteaded in Colorado and later moved to the wilderness of Idaho. Grandmas love to tell stories and little boys love to listen. To go with the stories, Grandma made beautiful head dresses from pheasant feathers. I learned how to make a bow from a bent willow branch and arrows from cattail reeds. As far back as I can remember we were playing cowboys and Indians. I have a picture of myself at the age of three wearing a black cowboy hat and packing a toy pistol. When given a choice I always opted to be an Indian. Though politically incorrect today, it was great fun tying up my little sisters and pretending to scalp them. Chief Joseph of the Nez Perce was one of my heroes. The aborted flight to freedom of his tribe was so sad. The idea of the *noble savage* was different in the 1950s. Once we got our television, I would take Tonto over the Lone Ranger any day. The Lone Ranger was okay, but you never saw him riding bareback, tracking an outlaw, or fighting with a knife; and Tonto could use sign language. I soon learned how to hold up my right hand as a sign of peace and say, "How."

Grandma figured that every boy needs to know how to shoot a gun, ride a horse, and catch a fish. She made it her mission to make "men" out of her grandsons. One summer she loaded Bill, me, and my cousins, Pat and Mike, into her 1950 Pontiac Streamliner. It was an ugly old thing with a yellowish paint job called San Pedro Ivory. The only thing I liked about it was the hood ornament, an amber colored Pontiac Indian head. We drove to a bleak area of sand dunes, sage brush, and cheat grass to catch lizards. What does this have to do with hunting and fishing? Well, if you can track and catch a lizard, you can track and catch just about anything. We surrounded a large clump of sage; Grandma beat the bush with a stick; and lizards ran in all directions. Our job was to catch them. Once you had your lizard, you tied a string to his tail and pinned it to your shirt. Looks real cool having a lizard ride around on your shoulder or stick its head out of your pocket. If you accidentally pulled off the tail, not a problem. It would grow back. Grandma claimed that lizards made great pets. I had my doubts. Whenever one came scurrying my way I put on a valiant show of trying to catch it, but it always got away. Those things, along with frogs, toads, and snakes give me the creeps. I can handle tadpoles, but not a big frog. My mom said that if it pees on you, you'll get warts.

Snakes were another story. Seemed our farm had more than its share. The black snakes would follow behind the plow catching worms when dad worked the fields. Bull snakes regularly showed up in the yard hoping to invade the chicken coop for an egg. We found their shed skins in the grassy fields. I remember finding one that stretched the entire length of our truck dash. The skins are like thin paper and somewhat delicate. We sometimes tacked them to a shed wall and threw knives at them. When you hit a skin with a pointed blade, it cuts apart and falls to the ground.

One time while hiking with my cousins along an irrigation canal, we came across a slither of garter snakes. There were dozens of them all wrapped up in a big ball. Soon Bill, Mike, and Pat had a snake in each hand. If you hold one just behind the head, it will coil around your wrist like an ancient Egyptian bracelet. I only held one that day, and Pat had to catch it for me. I couldn't let on that I was afraid. That would have invited torture. You never show fear to your cousins!

Grandma had lived as a teenager in the wilderness of Idaho south of Lewiston. Every summer she made a trip into the back country near New Meadows to share her teenage adventures with me and Bill. In the mornings we boys filled our individual Band-Aid tins with a handful of worms and headed to a small creek near our cabin. That's where I learned to tie hooks, clean fish, and improvise. If we ran out of worms, we collected periwinkles, small little grubs that live in tiny pods of sand along the gravelly banks. I also carried a couple fishing flies. A small black fly slowly reeled upstream from hole to hole will often produce a fish. Any fish we kept had to be at least six inches long. Brook trout don't get very big, and we were allowed to catch six a day. Grandma fried those little fish with the heads on so it would look like they filled the frying pan. She used so much lard that they were "deep fried" and crispy. We ate the skin and tails along with the flesh peeled from the ribs and backbone. When we finished a meal, there were four or five little skeletons stretched out on each plate. I thought it would be cool to mount one on a board and put it on my wall, but I never got around to it.

One summer Grandma took us to McCall, Idaho on the Payette Lakes. She had access to a small boathouse. While Bill and I swam, fished, and explored, Grandma suntanned and read books from a fenced deck on the roof. This was where I built my first squirrel trap. It was basically a box with a screen at one end and a sliding door at the other. When a squirrel took the bait, a string released a tiny stick holding the door and "bingo," you had a pet squirrel. We never did catch one, but I still have a scar on my left knee where I slipped while sawing a board.

Lake fishing was harder than creek fishing. The water was so clear you could see the bottom, which was about twelve feet deep at the edge of the boathouse. Little perch swam around the pilings, but we wanted a lake trout. We cast lures of every color and size. No luck. Bill's jar of salmon eggs finally did the trick but not in the way you would expect. I accidentally knocked the open jar off the deck. We watched its lazy descent while Bill called me a "stupid idiot." When the jar hit the bottom, the eggs gently rolled into the gravel and weeds. Fish oil drifted in whorls and swirls as the jar emptied.

First thing the next morning we ran to the deck and peered into the water. A half dozen humungous trout circled the jar. Several others lay among the weeds, glutted with salmon eggs. This was our chance, but do you think they would bite? Not on your life! We tried more salmon eggs. We tried worms. We dangled little red and white fishing lures in front of their noses. No interest. Finally Bill snagged a monster. The fight was on. Neither of us knew how to play a big fish but Bill managed to get it to the surface. I grabbed the net. I hate being the netter. Netters always get blamed when fish get away. Of course, I fumbled the net, and the trout threw the hook. Bill called me names that he had learned from my Uncle Lee. It's no wonder I lack self-esteem. We never did catch a trout from the platform of the boathouse.

Part of the experience at McCall was the outhouse. Apart from the smell and the flies, this one was very nice. The toilet seat was embossed with "Ladies be Seated." When you flipped up the lid, it read, "Goodie, Goodie, Daddy's Home". The walls were covered with funny postcards. One I still quote said,

Do you remember when you were a
wee, wee tot
And they took you from your warm, warm cot
And they sat you on that cold, cold pot

And they told you to go wee wee, whether you could or not?

GUNS WERE AN important part of our culture. I was seven or eight years old when Dad proudly brought home a new bolt action 16-gauge Mossberg shotgun. It was placed on a gun rack by the kitchen door along with a .22 rifle and a Russian 7.62. The shotgun was always handy in case some unsuspecting pheasant wandered across the back pasture.

I was too young to have a "real" gun, but I had a BB gun. Every boy I knew had one. We were good shots. How good, you say? We practiced until we could shoot over our shoulders using a mirror and hit a target behind us. One of the stupid things we did was lining up .22 cartridges along a crack in a log with the lead bullets stuffed into the crack and the rims facing out. Since the .22 cartridge is a rim-fire, when a bb hit the rim, the cartridge exploded. It never dawned on us that the empty case would come whizzing back at us. Thankfully, nobody was ever hit.

Some things I blame on Bill, but I was a willing participant. My dad had worked for several years at The Marshall Company, a local business that manufactured church furniture. Every night he brought home the sweepings from the daily cleanup. He sorted the screws and plugs into pint jars that neatly lined a shelf in our shop. Bill and I managed to shoot every one of them. *What were we thinking?* When we finished the jars, we started on the windows. Dad came home that night to find shelves strewn with little heaps of screws and glass. Any windows not shattered were pockmarked with tiny bb holes. My BB gun disappeared that night. Years later I learned that it lies at the bottom of the old privy.

Since I no longer had a BB gun, Bill came up with the idea of making one. He showed me how to bend a bicycle spoke into the rough shape of a handgun. The barrel end had the nipple, which was reversed and screwed back on, leaving enough room for a small amount of shavings from a match. A shotgun bb could be tapped firmly into the open end. Hold it over a candle, and *pop!* It wasn't very accurate but worked like a charm. Lacking any common sense, we hid in an empty grain bin to shoot them. Imagine a tiny bb ricocheting back and forth off the walls. It was almost as stupid as smoking a homemade corncob pipe in the barn. Yet, most farm boys grow up with both eyes and there are amazingly few barn fires.

About this time, my Grandpa Allen died from a heart attack. He was only fifty-three years old. I guess all those cigarettes, along with a few other bad habits, had caught up with him. I must have made an impression of some kind, because he left me his BB pistol and a small pocketknife. Maybe I was the only grandchild that enjoyed watching dogs howl and hotfoot it as much as he did. I often think of him while sitting on my back steps with a beany flipper waiting for the neighborhood cat. If it weren't for the fact that the neighbor would call the police, I'd use a BB gun. I have one identical to the one Grandpa gave me. Incidentally, I've never actually hit the cat. But it hates being shot at and has learned to avoid our birdfeeder.

Looking back I think Sam Gribley might have enjoyed *my* side of the mountain.

Those hombres better watch out!

Mike, Terry (author), Pat, and Bill
Thirty minutes later these outfits were covered in calf manure. We weren't much at catching outlaws and even worse at riding baby steers.

WILD TURKEY

MY DAD TOOK me on my first hunting trip when I was ten years old. I didn't carry a rifle, but I was a good spotter and knew to keep quiet. That year we hunted in Owyhee County in Idaho's southwestern corner. If my memory serves me, the deer had overrun the county, and the state was allowing two animals per hunter.

Dad's friend, Buzz, had worked on his olive green '49 Chevy pickup for at least two weeks before the trip. The truck had a canvas canopy that reminded me of an army truck. Our cots, cooler, cook stove, and other gear were stored there. Because of carburetor issues we got a late start. It was near dark when we left and pitch black when we turned off the main road southeast of a ghost town named Silver City.

You can't see much that time of night driving through semi-dessert terrain. There's not much to see in the daytime – mainly just cheat grass, sagebrush, and sand. We passed a parked truck or a dim campfire about every mile. When Buzz pulled off at the end of the road, all was dark and quiet. The men set up the cots in the back of the truck and we crawled into our warm sleeping bags; mine was a mummy bag that left only my eyes, nose, and mouth exposed.

A little before sunrise we woke to the rattle of pots and pans. Two cars and a truck were parked at a campsite not a hundred yards from us. Eight or ten people were milling around with their coffee mugs and tin plates. Buzz hadn't seen their camp in the dark. Our leisurely hunting trip was beginning to look like a fishing derby. The Coleman stove soon hissed a blue flame. The smell of coffee perking in the pot, bacon sizzling on the grill, and eggs sputtering in the pan filled the crisp morning air. When breakfast ended, Buzz began laboring on the Chevy to ensure our trip home. Funny thing, he knew some of the same words as my Uncle Lee.

Dad and I donned our fall jackets and red hunting hats. He shouldered his rifle, and I strapped a small bowie knife to my belt. It was time to find a nice little whitetail buck. The frost was melting on the trail as the sun peaked over the horizon. Rolling hills, rocky outcrops, and the occasional ravine were perfect for deer hunting. A sprinkling of pine graced the hills, and willows lined the creek beds. A Red-tailed hawk spiraled in the azure sky. I guess he was hunting for some hapless rabbit or sage hen, maybe even a lizard or a snake. Dark clouds hovered far to the west. Hiking up an outcropping, we passed the mouth of a cave. Animal tracks led in and out. Old dry ribs of some unfortunate deer lay in a heap beside the opening.

Dried rabbit hair clung to the surrounding brush. Dad said it was probably an old coyote den. I wanted to explore the inside, but we had more important things to do – like get a deer.

By mid-morning a buck and four does crested the hill above us. Dad was soon gutting a nice forked-horn buck. He had the most interesting hunting knife. The handle was made from antler and a bone saw was cut into the spine. It was wicked looking and so sharp that my dad could shave with the cutting edge. I would have tried it, but at ten I was more likely to cut my lip or nick my nose than find a whisker. Dad had his buck tagged and field dressed in a jiffy. He pointed out the liver and heart to me and explained why you take great care not to cut into the stomach or the guts. Then he pulled a thermos and two sandwiches from his pack. That was the life!

Just as I bit into a thick slice of baloney, a six-point buck topped the ridge and trotted down the hill toward us.

"Dad," I said. "Look! Can I shoot him?"

"Sure, let's see what you can do."

I picked up his rifle, chambered a shell, and raised it to my shoulder. My dad's rifle, an old Russian 7.62 from World War I, might be termed a poor man's "deer gun." The length of those things was forty-eight and a half inches, over eight inches longer than the average hunting rifle. It was deadly accurate, but hard to steady by a little guy like me. The end of the barrel was bobbing up and down and weaving back and forth, pointing at everything but that deer.

The buck spotted me and turned; I fired; the deer stumbled and fell; and I plummeted onto my back, the rifle flying end over end into a clump of sagebrush. Had I known about recoil, I'd have been afraid to pull the trigger. That old gun kicked like a mule. Dad stood over me with the biggest grin you ever saw. "Are you okay?" He held out a hand. "Great shot."

As I regained my feet, a hunter appeared at the top of the hill and shouted, "Did you see my buck? It ran this direction about thirty seconds ago." He spotted the deer, ran down the bluff, and pulled out his knife.

Dad said, "Wait a minute. My son shot that deer."

"Really?" He replied. "How do you explain that my tag is attached to the antlers?"

At the time, deer tags in Idaho were made from a strip of metal that clipped together around the horns or a rib. Once attached, only wire cutters or tin snips would take one off. There it was, wrapped around the base of one antler, all bright and shiny.

My dad looked at the buck and examined the tag. "Well," he stammered. "I guess if you ran fast enough to tag it, we'll have to let you have it."

"But Dad–"

The hunter interrupted. "Here's the hole where I shot him...right here. I walked up and tagged him and as I pulled out my knife the darned thing started kicking, jumped up, and took off. You can see where it clipped me in the leg."

"But Dad–"

"–Sorry boy," the man continued. "I shot him, and I tagged him. There's no other hole. Unless you think you scared him to death, he's mine."

BUZZ WAS FRYING fresh liver and onions when we reached camp. He'd fixed the carburetor on the Chevy and by mid-morning had a nice little whitetail of his own hanging from an old juniper that graced our campsite. He was happily bellowing an off-key rendition of "Hey, Good Looking" as we approached.

Sharing a meal with Dad and Buzz was the closest thing I could imagine to sitting beside God and Jesus, though surely there's no liver in heaven. I needed a quarter cup of ketchup to get mine down. We sat beside the fire as they swapped lies about past hunting trips. They each popped open a Coors and lit a cigar. I sat sipping a cup of hot chocolate.

Buzz winked at my dad and looked at me. "Did I ever tell ya about the day I bagged two deer with one shot? I reckon it was the best day of huntin' I ever had, or ever will. I was grouse huntin' in the early fall just below Pouthena Falls where Asteio Creek disappears into the wilderness. I had worn my hip waders and packed a folding fishing rod in case the birds were scarce. I always like to bring somethin' home to Momma. That particular day I was packing my over and under .30-30/20 gauge. It's a dandy little rifle and good for birds or bucks. You can't be too prepared.

"It was a magnificent fall day. The leaves on the birch and aspens were turning to gold and vermillion. Indian paintbrush, that's my favorite plant, waved along the creek bank. I'd come across bear track and coyote scat. The bears were some fat that year. I sat on a stump enjoyin' a cup of coffee from my thermos near the spot where I shot my first snowshoe rabbit. It was actually a snowshoe hare. There's a difference between rabbits and hares. Rabbits are born without a stitch of fur and with their eyes closed. Hares, on the other hand, come into the world fully clothed and eyes wide open. They're tough – just like me and your daddy. Summertime finds a hare wearing a brindle brown fur coat that blends with the forest. In winter it changes into fluffy white camo. I wouldn't have seen that one if it hadn't turned color early. Nearly jumped out of my boots when what looked like a giant piece of white fluff jumped from a green patch of juniper. I guess old fluffy didn't realize he had changed color, because he only hopped a few yards before turning to check me out. Shot him right through the eye with the .30-30. Now that's good shootin'!

"Anyway, getting' back to the story. It was so still I could hear a leaf settle on the ground where it fell from a nearby birch. Pebbles faintly rumbled along the bottom of the creek. A squirrel chattered away, concerned about my presence in his territory. When you're in the wilderness, just sit and listen sometime. You'll be surprised at what ya hear. I sat gazin' into a pool below a large log that poked out about ten feet into the creek. Fish often lurk in the shade of old logs.

"The ear of a little spike buck flicking back and forth caught my attention. A deer was nibbling on a wild rosebush on the other side of the creek. Boy oh boy! It was the perfect size. Then I noticed a second buck standing behind the first. It looked like a twin. Boy oh boy! If I got into the right position, I might get both with one shot. Now that would be somethin'! Down went my pole and up came my rifle. Inch by inch I slid one foot after the other along the slippery surface of that log until I lined one deer directly behind the other. So far, so good. I aimed and fired. There's not much kick to a .30-30 but just enough to knock me off the log and into the cold chest-deep pool. My waders quickly filled with water and would have pulled me under if it had been any deeper. Many a man's drowned that way. I held my gun above the water with my right hand and flailed away with the left as I scrambled to the opposite bank. Boy, oh boy was I lucky! When I staggered onto the bank, both of my hip waders went into convulsions. I quickly pulled them off and poured out thirteen little brook trout. Can you believe that? Thirteen! Then I stepped into the brush to see if I'd hit anything. There was my deer and right behind it was its twin. Two deer with one shot!

"I always look for the bullet hole so I can grade my shooting. This time I was spot on. I could see where the slug went into the first deer and where it came out. I looked and looked at the second but couldn't find a hole. Finally I notice a splash of blood and a smitch of white where the slug had ricocheted just behind its left antler. The concussion musta done him in. About that time a pinecone thumped me on the head. Lookin' up, I saw a swath of broken branches along one side of a tall pine. Boy oh boy! A humungous black bear lay at the base of the tree. The bullet had glanced off the deer and struck old Smokey[1] through the heart. And that

---

[1] Smokey Bear was part of a U.S. Forest Service advertising campaign to help prevent forest fires. As a little boy I often ran around the yard singing: "Smokey the Bear, Smokey the Bear, prowlin' and a growlin' and a sniffin' the air. He can find a fire before it starts to flame. That's why

wasn't the end of it. When I rolled the bear over, there was a rabbit, laid out flat as a pancake.

"I have to say, that was the best day of huntin' I ever had: thirteen trout, two deer, one bear, and a rabbit. All bagged with only one shot. And by golly that's the truth or St. Peter wasn't a cowboy."

My eyes were as big as two shiny quarters.

I looked at my dad and said, "I never knew St. Peter was a cowboy."

"Well, now you know," he replied. "Now finish your hot chocolate and get into that sleeping bag. We have a big day coming up tomorrow."

I WOKE TO the sound of voices, the crackle of the fire, and a whiff of bacon. The rest of our party had arrived sometime during the night. My mom had hitched a ride with Buzz's parents, Bert and Heather. Buzz's brother had also come. Their friends, Frank and Angela Cummins, brought their '55 Ford F-1. It was my kind of truck – barn red with a white roof. Might be needed for all those deer we were going to bag. Some folks were checking their rifles and ammunition. Others were enjoying a hot, steaming cup of camp coffee. Similar sounds drifted from across the way, a reminder that we were not alone.

I was sitting on the tailgate of Buzz's Chevy pulling on my socks when a herd of deer crested the knoll above our camp and trotted straight toward us. "Look!" I yelled. "Deer!" The herd picked up speed and

---

they call him Smokey, that was how he got his name." It was an effective campaign.

bounded directly between the two camps. Someone started shooting and pandemonium broke loose as volleys of gunfire erupted from both camps. Women were screaming. Men were cussing. I dodged behind a boulder as fourteen deer ran the gauntlet. When the rifle smoke cleared, guess how many animals were shot? You guessed it. Not one!

Bert Richards rolled up his sleeves, clenched his fists, and stomped toward the other camp. "By golly someone needs to learn a lesson!" A burly-looking fellow in a red plaid jacket met him halfway. The muffled cussing and swearing curled my ears as I heard words I had never heard before. They never did agree on who fired the first shot. I think both men were downright embarrassed at what had happened. It's a good thing no one actually hit a deer. They'd still be arguing.

Back to business. My mom hurried through the breakfast cleanup and threw together a few sandwiches for our tramp into the hills. Then she picked up a Lee Enfield she had borrowed from an old timer named Klaus who lived down the road from our farm. She began fiddling with the bolt and trigger action: out and in, click; out and in, click; out and in, click. "Come on you guys. Hurry up. We haven't got all day." Mom didn't often get off the farm. She always claimed to be a crack shot and was hoping to prove it by bagging her first deer.

We followed the trail that Dad and I had taken the day before. As morning advanced, the temperature dropped, the wind picked up, and clouds filled the sky. A light snow soon covered the trail. Fresh deer tracks crossing the path ahead of us led to a clump of willows at the bottom of a steep gully. Dad posted mom beside a large boulder. I followed him as he hiked in a large semi-circle intending to come to the willows from the opposite side. He planned to drive the animals out of the thicket and up the hill to my mom. But the wind picked up and soon howled over the ridge and through the bluffs. Heavy blowing snow reduced visibility to ten yards, ending any chance of seeing a deer. Our own tracks quickly disappeared in the drifting snow. We trekked back to my mom. It was time to get back to camp while patches of the trail were still visible. I recognized the mouth of the coyote den as we passed and wondered if anything was hiding in there.

We were the last of our group to return to camp and joined the others in the back of Buzz's truck. It reminded me of soldiers crammed into the back of a troop carrier. A full-fledged blizzard shrieked outside and the truck canvas flapped and groaned in protest. Fred Cummins pulled out a bottle of Wild Turkey bourbon and passed it around. All eyes focused on me as Dad handed me the bottle – I was only ten and the only kid there. I was wet and cold and beginning to shiver. I looked at that bottle, took a swig, and nearly did a back flip. I could hardly catch my breath. Mr. Cummins was laughing. Bert Richards guffawed, "Reckon he's a hunter alright!"

The back canvas flap suddenly jerked open and a man's face appeared. His eyebrows and mustache were frosted with snow. His cheeks were red with cold. "A woman from our party is missing," he said. "Any of you folks come across her? She was on the main trail going west." Everyone shook their heads.

My dad said, "We came back that way and didn't see anyone."

I thought about how our tracks disappeared in the falling snow and was happy to be in the back of that pickup.

There was no radio reception and no way of knowing how long the storm would last. The wind howled through the gullies and around the rocky outcrops. Snow was piling up by the minute. It would soon be impossible to drive out. Time to load and go. By the time we reached the town of Murphy local authorities had closed the main highway. The blizzard lasted four more days and the roads into the wilderness were impassable for the rest of the winter.

The missing woman's body was found four months later. Remember the cave I wanted to explore? She had sheltered there to wait out the storm.

THE FOLLOWING YEAR, Dad took me hunting in the mountains near New Meadows, Idaho. The group included my Uncle Lee, Bill, and a guy named Charlie Butler. Uncle Lee brought his pack horses. This was Bill's first hunting trip. I was still too young to carry a rifle, but I appreciate that my dad included me on those outings.

Charlie was a funny guy and full of stories and pranks. For his honeymoon he'd taken his wife into the wilderness where they stayed for six months while he worked a trapline: no electricity, no television or radio, few books, and no other people. That would unhinge most folks. He and his wife had just adopted two little Korean boys. He said that every night Mrs. Butler would tuck them snuggly under the covers, and every morning she would find them sleeping on the cold floor. They weren't used to a bed and blankets. Just before Charlie joined us for the trip, his oldest son had said, "Daddy, bring me back a bear!"

Charlie had Bill and me believing that we talked to each other in our sleep. Our first night the conversation supposedly went like this.

Bill: "Fish...fishh...fishhhh..."

Terry: "Where?"

Bill: "There...therrrrr..."

Terry: "Where?"

Bill: "You fool, you broke your pole!"

I was skeptical. "We didn't, did we?"

He grinned, "Ask your dad. The two of you got to carrying on so bad, you woke everybody up. And what was that about breaking your pole?"

As Charlie was speaking, the fire crackled in the old cast-iron stove. Coffee bubbled and perked in a blue ceramic pot. Strips of bacon sizzled and hissed in a large iron skillet. Uncle Lee was outside saddling the packhorses, Scout and Gypsy. Bill and I forked down our breakfast, threw on our coats, and charged out the door.

The track we followed that day had been used a month earlier by Basque shepherds. In the early summer they move their sheep to the mountain meadows as the lower pastures turn yellow from the desert heat. In the fall, the flocks are returned to the home ranches where they shelter and feed through the winter. I once saw a shepherd with a small, covered wagon, a mule, a dog, and a flock of Targhees[2] just beginning his trek into the mountains. Sure looked like fun.

Uncle Lee led the way, followed by Bill; Charlie came next, leading Scout; then my dad with Gypsy; and last in line, yours truly. The trail followed creeks and waterfalls as it wended up a deep canyon. We were hiking along a narrow ridge when a sharp-tailed grouse burst from the brush. Gypsy shied and started bucking. In the blink of an eye she lost her footing and began a rapid slide down the loose scree of the canyon wall. In horror I watched my dad clutch Gypsy's halter with one hand and claw at the loose gravel with his other hand in a desperate attempt to avoid tumbling to the bottom of the ravine. Horse and handler skidded to a stop fifty feet below the trail. My dad calmed Gypsy and gingerly led her back to our group.

As we hiked on, I asked, "Dad, why didn't you let go of Gypsy when she stumbled?"

"Well, son," he replied. "If I hadn't gone with her, she probably would have rolled and fallen all the way to the bottom. We would have lost all our gear, and more importantly, we would have lost a good horse. I was determined not to let her go unless I had to."

Many years later while reading Psalm 23, "Yeah, though I walk through the valley of the shadow of death, I will fear no evil; For you are with me..." I remembered my dad and how he stayed with that horse.

---

[2] Targhees are a breed of sheep developed in Idaho in the 1920s.

Cresting into the mountain meadows, we stopped at a roughhewn sheepfold situated near a fresh spring. It was the perfect place to tether the horses. Then our party split, Uncle Lee, Bill, and Charlie going one direction, and Dad and me going another.

My spotting was superb that day. Dad and I came across deer after deer, and he fired shot after shot but no luck. I remember pointing to a good-sized buck that was peering out from the trees.

"It's right there, Dad. Can't you see it?"

"Where?"

"There."

"You take the rifle. I couldn't hit the broadside of a barn today."

"Now it's gone." I breathed a sigh of relief. After my last experience with that old 7.62, I wasn't ready to try it again. Spotting was good enough for me.

We met up with the others late in the day. They hadn't seen a thing. I suspect it's because of all the visiting and cigarette smoke from Uncle Lee and Charlie. Deer weren't born with big ears for nothing, and they have a healthy fear of smoke. Meanwhile my dad had been ruminating about all the shots he'd missed. He couldn't believe his shooting could be that bad. A deer is a relatively big target. He hadn't felt a need to sight his rifle for the trip, but just maybe..." He marked a patch on a corral post and paced off twenty-five yards.[3] *Blam!* Bark splintered from a pine to the

---

[3] Some fellows I know site their rifles in at a hundred yards. That requires a good spotter scope or a lot of leg work. I sight mine in at twenty-five yards. Bullets travel in an arch rather than a straight line. At twenty-five yards the slug is in an upward trajectory that will arch and descend to the

left of the post. He shot again, this time at a horizontal plank. *Kapow!* The bullet buried itself over six inches to the left of his aim. That's over two feet off center at a hundred yards. The good news: it wasn't his aim. The bad news: his front sight had struck a rock when he slid down the canyon wall with Gypsy. It was no wonder he couldn't hit anything. He readjusted the sight but any opportunity to drop a buck was gone.

Back at camp that evening a couple weary young lads scoffed down steak and fried potatoes, then headed to the bath hut. The pungent smell of sulfur led to a bricked tub of steaming mineral water. *Ouch, oo, ow,* the water was hot. We splashed, soaped up, and made a general mess of things. Then we lifted a plank on one side of the tub and the dirty water flowed out and fresh, hot, spring water flowed in. There was no talking in our sleep that night.

---

same height at one hundred yards. It makes for a quick adjustment on a scope or open sight.

DAFFY DUCKS

BUZZ CAME TO visit my dad on a Friday night that December. I was in the kitchen snacking on Sugar Pops and heard them talking and laughing in the front room. The room went quiet, and Dad whispered, "You have to see what I got Swede (that was my nickname) for Christmas."

They disappeared into my parents' room, came out laughing, and went outside to work on Buzz's truck. I hightailed it into that bedroom. Nothing behind the door. Nothing under the bed. A long box, about four feet tall, four inches deep, and eight inches wide stood in the corner of the closet partially hidden by an old grey suit. I looked out the window to make sure they were still in the shop. Then I quickly brought out the box and laid it on the bed. Inside was a new Marlin bolt action .410 shotgun. I gingerly removed it from the box and brought it to my shoulder. Perfect. Then I carefully placed it back in the box and returned it to the closet.

That night while we were eating, conversation centered on Santa Claus. Keep in mind that gifts were minimal in our family. Christmas time was about the only time we had oranges or bananas. Given a bag of oranges, my little sister, Vicki, and I would keep eating till we broke out in a rash. A couple books, a pocketknife, and a year's worth of socks were pretty standard gifts for me. A Barbie and a toy nursing kit suited Vicki. I did get a wind-up train one year. I broke the spring on the first wind and never did see it run. Sometimes we received a game like Chinese Checkers that could be enjoyed by the whole family. Gifts tended to be on the practical side. I suspected that my parents played "Santa" but always professed to be a true believer in the old fellow. Mom said that when you stop believing, he stops coming.

Dad finished wiping his plate clean with a buttered piece of bread and looked at me. "What would you like Santa to bring this year?"

I innocently looked at my plate and then up to the ceiling. "A gun would be nice."

"You looked, you little bugger!"

I had to wait for Santa to arrive on Christmas morning and act surprised when the .410 appeared. Vicki was a strong believer in old Saint Nick, and I was told that if I slipped the secret, a wash rag and lumps of coal would appear in my Christmas stocking.

That shotgun became my joy. Through spring and summer old cans had to suffice for practice. Finally September arrived and the bird season opened. Dinah crept into her space under the house, and I headed to the fields. The only birds I ever shot with that gun were some helpless little mourning doves. The first one was sitting on a telephone wire that ran to our house. The poor thing was calling, *coo, coo, coo-oo-oo-oo*. It was an easy shot; still, I only winged it. It sat on the ground blinking its mournful eyes at me. I nearly cried, and I'm certain I would have if the phone line had snapped. *What was I thinking?* However, my temporary remorse didn't deter me from shooting another one.

When the ducks arrived, I was convinced my time had come. Hundreds, maybe thousands, landed in the stubble behind our house. You've heard the phrase, "dumb duck." Well, I've never met one. I'll wager that the fellow who says, "it was like shooting ducks in a barrel," never came across a group of ducks stupid enough to swim in a barrel. As soon as you get within thirty or forty yards they fly away. Experts say the .410 is good from twenty-five to forty yards. Not in my experience. Nonetheless, you have to be sneaky, which is impossible when crawling through five-inch stubble in an open wheat field.

There was a small irrigation pond about a mile from our house that attracted fifteen or twenty ducks at a time. A heavy clump of cattails bordered the south side. If I walked right up to it there wouldn't be a duck in sight by the time I arrived. So I walked past on the road as if going somewhere else – ducks seem to fall for that ploy – and then cut across the field behind the willows. Crawling army-style, I slithered through the grass that lay behind the reeds. It was a tactic I learned from our tomcat. I took my time, crawling two or three feet and then pausing. "One, one thousand...two, one thousand...three, one thousand..." I'd count off ten seconds, then crawl ahead. I couldn't see them, but I knew they were there. *Cackle, cackle, quack, quack, splash, splash.* Ducks love to carry on while eating. When I reached the cattails, I carefully parted a half dozen stalks. Suddenly everything was quiet as a tomb. I peered through. Fifteen ducks gawped back. I lifted my gun. Fifteen ducks lifted their bodies off the water and into the sky. By the time I flipped off the safety and looked down the barrel there was nothing on the water but a few ripples and a scattering of scraggly feathers.

Klaus Reimers and his wife, Frieda, were like surrogate grandparents to me and Vicki. They lived about five miles down the road from us in a huge brick house. The bricks were beginning to crumble, and the upstairs had been sealed off. A screened veranda held a large bed that they used on hot summer nights. Klaus loved fishing and wild berry picking. He occasionally dropped a gunnysack full of croppies or bluegills at our house. My mom figured it was his way of getting out of cleaning the little things. Some folks are more into the catching than into the eating. One Saturday night we were invited to their place for supper. I was explaining my duck hunting woe over a piece of boysenberry pie. Vicki thought it was "poisonberry" and wouldn't eat hers. Klaus, with his strong German accent, said, "I show you how to hunt ducks. You and your *vati* come with me."

Klaus retrieved his pump 12-gauge and led us to a strip of field corn beside his barn. The sun had set two hours earlier and you couldn't see a thing, but there was no mistaking that *cackle, cackle, quack, quack.* A regular mallard hootenanny was taking place in that corn patch.

"You will keep behind me, yah?" he said. Then he aimed at a thirty-degree angle toward the ground. *BOOM!* Wings and cackle accompanied a squadron of mallards scrambling from the corn patch. Klaus raised the barrel to eye level. *BOOM!* He then aimed into a mass of confusing shadows rising above the corn. *BANG!* "You come tomorrow for breakfast. I show you ducks!"

The next morning we arrived at 6:30. I could hardly contain myself, but Klaus was in no hurry. He wouldn't begin his day without his coffee and streusel. He assured me the ducks weren't going anywhere. I have to admit, a tall glass of fresh cow's milk and a hot apple turnover from Frieda's oven gives a boy a pleasant outlook on the day. Finally Klaus wiped the crumbs from his mouth and pushed back his chair. "Now I show you ducks!"

Things look different in the daylight. The ducks had done their damage to the corn. Stalks were broken, leaves torn, and cobs strewn on the ground. Klaus gave me a gunny sack and sent me into the corn patch while he smoked a cigarette and chatted with my dad. I started down a row: one duck; two ducks; three ducks. I moved to a second row: four ducks; five ducks. Third row: one dead Jersey calf that had strayed into the corn the night before. Klaus got a lot of meat with only three shots, but he was not happy. His final words to me on the matter, "Let that be a lesson about shooting in the dark!"[4]

After five years of crawling through stubble, hiding behind trees, and lurking in the cattails, I had shot a total of four mourning doves, one muskrat, and seventy-eight old beer cans. I never did master shotgun shooting.

Vicki, Dinah, and Terry – 1957
I had recently been hit between the eyes with a rock.

[4] My family attended church every Sunday. I had noticed that the Reimers didn't attend church and had to ask why. Klaus told me, "I try it once but later that day while cleaning fish under the tree by the barn, the lightning strike that tree. I figure it be a warning from the Devil and I promise him that I never go again!"

Terry, Red, and a school chum named Billy Fields

Dogs were an important part of growing up

THE CRAWDAD HOLE

MOM AND dad split the sheets when I was twelve, and my mom moved the family to Woodburn, Oregon. No one I knew was into fishing. WWSD, what would Sam do? I quickly discovered the Pudding River, aptly named after its chocolate-colored water. With my fishing gear strapped to an old bicycle I would ride past small farms and cornfields to a bridge that crosses the river about a mile and a half out the old Wilco Highway. I doubt that anyone else fished that river because of the drainage from local farms. Things like that don't enter your mind at age thirteen. I soon knew all the holes where fish lurked, even one or two where a rare trout was found.

We had lived in Woodburn for about a year when I talked a couple buddies, Vince and Ted, into camping overnight along the river. We rode to the bridge and hid our bikes in the weeds. Between us, we had two pup tents, our sleeping bags, and a pack of camp food. A pasture provided the perfect spot to pitch our tents near a bend in the river.

We had our fishing poles and a can of worms. Speaking of which, no thirteen-year-old alive would have paid for worms. I had gone out the night before and caught my own. The nightcrawlers come out after dark to "know" each other in the grass. It's kind of an Adam and Eve thing if you know what I mean. You find them with a flashlight. When you see the glint of a slimy body you quickly grab it before it zips back into the ground; then gently tug so as not to pull it apart. They put up a surprising fight. Old Mr. Moss, our neighbor, swore that on rainy nights the nightcrawlers wriggle up the clothesline poles and hang on the lines to keep from drowning. We had plenty of rain, but I never once found a worm dangling from the clothesline. Nonetheless, they're great for fishing. One nightcrawler will bait three or four hooks. Vince told me that they don't feel any pain. The way a worm fights going onto a hook makes me wonder.

I transformed an old coffee can into a crawdad trap. The open end was covered by wire mesh with a hole cut in the center for the crayfish to enter. Nail holes in the bottom of the can allowed the water to drain through. The idea was for the crayfish to crawl into the can to feast on some old chicken scraps and still be there when I pulled the makeshift trap from the water. I tied my contraption to a rope and launched it into the river before we set up camp. We also baited and set our lines. It's a lazy man's way to fish, but it fulfills the three basic rules of fishing: keep a worm on your hook; keep your line in the water; and be patient.

By early evening we hadn't had a nibble. My reputation was on the line, but what could I do? Ted was tending our little campfire. A rabbit, cut in pieces and ready for the frying pan, appeared from his pack. It put any fried chicken I've tasted to shame.

As the rabbit sizzled in the pan, I decided to check the crawdad trap. Guess what? Three little crayfish. They didn't look like the lobsters you see on restaurant signs. These were dark green, almost brown. Creepy looking little worms wriggled on their bodies and tails. We weren't the only ones looking for a meal. Vince and Ted took one look and swore off crayfish for life. I refused to be dissuaded. A kettle soon boiled over the fire. As long as something is boiled long enough, it won't kill you, right? Soon I dropped the little critters into the water. As the crawdads boiled, the worms fell off, and the shells turned a rich pinky-red. I removed them from the pot and snapped off the tails. The flesh inside was delicious! Reminded me of shrimp. Vince and Ted will never know what they missed, and that's fine by me.

The sun had set. Venus twinkled in the western horizon. Flames from the fire danced in the dark. Vince launched into a story about a rabid frog that attacked boys in their sleeping bags whenever a cloud covered the moon. Their long slimy tongues were said to slither down your ears and suck out your brains. Thankfully there were no clouds that night. I glanced at the moon and at its reflection on the water. Hot diggity dog! Ted's pole was whipping up and down like a flagpole in a hurricane. *Fish on!* A chubby little catfish was soon writhing around in the grass. We placed a camp lantern at the edge of the dark pool that swirled beside our campsite. So much for getting any sleep. The lantern drew the fish and the nightcrawlers did the rest.

I had a fish stringer, the kind where each fish has a giant safety pin clipped through its gills. With one end of the stringer attached to a bush or around a rock, you can keep live fish in the water. That way they stay fresh and don't dry out. I checked my stringer every so often. About midnight I held the lantern close to the water. What the...? The tail was missing from the first fish on the stringer. I looked closer. The biggest crawdad – so big it was like a mobster lobster – had a humungous claw locked onto the second fish and was trying to drag it away. Good thing I looked. Can you imagine pulling up a stringer only to find a dozen fish skeletons? After that I kept a regular watch over our catch. By morning we had a dozen nice catfish. Most of mine still had the hook lodged in their mouths where I had cut the line. I just couldn't bring myself to touch those whiskers.

I WAS AT that stage of life when girls are "yucky." Who needed them? My little sister Vicki didn't agree. She nagged and nagged and nagged to go fishing with me. I finally relented. We rode our bikes to a fairly open riverbank along the Pudding. I had only one pole and I wasn't about to share it. So I rigged up a long willow branch with a line, bobber, and hook for Vicki that would only reach about two feet from the bank. It was unlikely to catch a fish but as long as she was happy, I could get on with some serious fishing. My spin caster would reach almost three quarters across the river. A *green frog* Len Thompson spoon was bound to hook a nice bass. I cast and cast. Nothing. Meanwhile Vicki had her line in the water, out of the water, snagged in a bush, back in the water. She laid down her pole and took a break to make a chain necklace from dandelion stems. I yelled at her for trying to skip stones on the water. "Don't you know nuthin'? You'll never catch a fish that way! Fishing is serious business." It's no wonder boys keep girls out of their inner circle. Girls are entirely too relaxed.

"I got one! I got one!" Vicki's pole was bent almost double. Would have broken right off if it hadn't been a fresh willow branch. Since there's no reel on a willow pole, you either back up until you drag the fish onto the bank, or you lift the pole until you can grab the line and bring it in hand over hand. She chose the latter method and soon had the nicest small-mouthed bass you ever saw. It had been hiding in the weeds about a foot from the bank where she happened to drop her line while studying a water bug. That's another good reason not to take a girl fishing. She'll humiliate you every time.

MOM WORKED NIGHT and day to keep food on the table and clothes on our backs. She loved the ocean and on rare occasions made a trip to Tillamook where my Grandma Allen owned a cottage. Mom one time paid for me and a friend named John to spend a morning salmon fishing out of Depoe Bay. The weather was cold; the sky was overcast and drizzly; and the ocean was dark and rough. We boarded a four-hour charter and were sicker than dogs for three hours and fifty-five minutes. John and I each covered ourselves with a small tarp for protection from the rain and wind. Our heads hung over the rail, and we upchucked non-stop the whole time. I seriously considered jumping overboard to end my misery. I had two or three hits over the four hours, but no salmon. John never even bothered to check his pole. As soon as we returned past the breakwater and into the bay, the vomiting ceased. It was like a miracle. The skipper felt bad for us and offered to take us free of charge on his next run. We scrambled off that boat like rats fleeing a sinking ship. I've gone ground fishing out of Depoe Bay several times since, but always take a double dose of Gravol before stepping off the dock.

Next time to the coast I tried jetty fishing. A bait shop sold long bamboo poles with a single eyelet on the tip. I bought a spool of line, a half-dozen one-ounce weights, a package of hooks, and a bag of shrimp. I secured the line at the base of the rod and ran a long length up and out the eye. A weight and hook were positioned at the end. It happened that the tide was going out and just about to turn, perfect timing. From a safe perch on the rocks, I threw the line as far as I could. The pole gently bowed up and down in tandem with the tide, then went crazy. A sea bass had taken the bait. Two more bass and three blue rockfish later, I considered myself a seasoned ocean fisherman. A sculpin changed that mental image. I have never seen a scarier fish. This one could have been a finned demon from Dante's Inferno come to get me. It leered at me with a wide ugly grin; horns jutted from its head; large pectoral fins fanned out like a bully waving his fingers with his thumbs stuck in his ears. The hook's still in that yucky old thing. I took it home to show my friends.

The last time I saw it, it was smiling from a large jar of formaldehyde where I left it when we moved from Woodburn.

I GAVE UP ocean vessels for a number of years, but I never gave up hope of catching a salmon. I recall fishing on the Tillamook River from a rocky bluff that overhung a deep pool. It was the perfect spot. An oversized treble hook loaded with a gob of salmon eggs and wrapped like a mummy with red thread was certain to do the trick. I cast into the top of the pool and let it slowly drift down – again and again and again. If I'd caught something I don't know how I'd have gotten it out of the water. A net was the furthest thing from my mind and my eight-pound test line was not made for salmon.

I was having no luck, but I was fascinated by a mutant frog that was swimming near shore. A miniature frog was growing out of the back of a large, speckled croaker that was lazily drifting down the river. They seemed to be paddling in tandem. It was the strangest thing I'd ever seen. It was twenty years before it dawned on me that it might have been some kind of mating ritual, and another thirty-five years before I read about how frogs have babies. Those things weren't talked about back in the day. Back to fishing. I packed up my gear as an older man stepped onto the same outcrop. Six casts later, he took home two large, silver-colored salmon. I wish I had paid attention to how he did that.

A real fisherman never reveals a good spot. Leak the location even once and the trails will look like a freeway within a couple years. Somewhere in Oregon I came upon a still pool with what I think were fifty or more sockeye. Whatever they were, they were a dull red color and coming to the end of their spawn. When you're thirteen years old you don't pay attention to the species, and you're not concerned with the regulations. You just want to catch a fish. I opened my tackle box and worked my way through every lure I owned, but no luck.

I eventually gave up and hiked upstream to a rocky outcrop above a large, deep pool where a stream of bubbles rippled from the bottom of the river. I watched as the bubbles slowly circled around the pool. Down went the tackle box and out came a large red and white spoon. *Must be a monster. Probably a chinook. Maybe today's the day!* I cast into the basin and slowly reeled across the trail of bubbles. The current pulled the lure off track. I cast again trying to gauge the current. No luck. And again and again and again.

The line went slack as bubbles gushed toward the surface of the water. A dark, round head appeared. *A seal, maybe?* Two large eyes slowly emerged. Then a hand appeared, dangling my lure between a thumb and forefinger. *A scuba diver!*

Sad to say, I had to wait another fifty years before finally hooking a salmon.

WHITETAILS

AT AGE FOURTEEN I saved enough money from berry picking to buy an army surplus rifle. Uncle Bob's Sporting Goods had several cases of Lee-Enfields. The fact that they had been used in two world wars made them all the more valuable to me. The .303 I chose had been packed in grease and stored for who knows how long. The stock was scratched and patched. The rifling was worn from hundreds, maybe thousands of rounds being fired. I didn't know what rifling was at the time or how to check the muzzle for wear. The butt end looked like it had been used to pound nails. It was well worn, which I thought was good thing. I wanted a rifle that had experience. I took it home and cleaned off the grease. To make it look like a *real* deer rifle, I whittled a pound or so off the stock and stained the wood a dark walnut. To be perfectly honest, it was pretty ugly. Whittling is not my thing. The rear site could be adjusted up and down with marks calibrated for up to two thousand yards. Can you imagine shooting at something over a mile away? A .303s trajectory is like a rainbow compared to a high-performance hunting rifle. Think of the arch a bullet would make going that distance? The old guns were fairly accurate if the target didn't move while waiting for the bullet. I guess that's why mountain men lick a forefinger and hold it up to gauge the wind before taking a long shot. A rifle that can group three shots within a one-inch circle at one hundred yards is effective out to three hundred yards. Whenever I sighted mine in, which generally meant a couple shots at a beer can on the way to the woods, I was happy if I could come within four inches at twenty-five yards. Believe it or not, I shot a lot of deer with that old gun.

That fall my dad phoned, "You wouldn't like to go deer hunting would you?"

"Oh, wouldn't I, wouldn't I!" I answered.

Once again, we rode with Buzz, this time in a 1960 Dodge pickup with no canopy. Frank and Angela Cummins led the way in their '53 Fargo up an old logging road in Central Oregon. A fire had gone through a few years before and the new growth was phenomenal. New lodgepole pine were springing up between the old stumps and blackened spruce. Pine grass covered the open areas. Fireweed with its lavender blooms bordered the road. The occasional clump of Indian paintbrush dotted the hillside. Yellow broadleaf arnica waved to us from between the fallen logs. Following a fire the new growth provides abundant seed and forage for birds and deer and other forest animals. We had entered deer country and expected to see a buck at every turn in the road.

Fred Cummin's brake lights came on just around the bend ahead of us. When the Fargo lurched to a stop, Buzz jammed on the breaks. "They musta seen somethin'," he said. Before my dad could step out of the truck, the passenger door on the Fargo opened and Angela jumped out with a roll of toilet paper. We watched as she maneuvered around a couple stumps and into the shrubs out of Fred's sight but fully in view of our truck. She loosened her belt and began to drop her pants.

Buzz looked at my dad and winked. "Looks like we're gonna see a little 'whitetail'."

Dad grinned and said, "I don't think so," and reached across and hit the horn.

Angela had her pants up in less time than a frog takes to flick a fly. She glared at us, waved her fist, and stomped back to the Fargo. She was the only "doe" we saw that morning.

The plan for the afternoon was to spread out and push through a large block of timber. I slowly stalked through the brush, walking five yards, counting to ten, then creeping forward another five yards. I saw tracks, but no deer. I came across piles of fresh droppings, but no deer. I identified the nibbled tips of wild roses, but no deer. Around four o'clock in the afternoon the rumps of four does appeared. Their little white tails were held high and waving "goodbye" as they quickly dissolved into the trees. Walk five yards, count to ten, walk five yards. There they were again. They moved. I moved. It was like a dance. I forgot all about meeting up with my dad and Buzz. As the sun waned, those little white tails flagged me deeper and deeper into the forest.

You ever get the feeling that something is watching you? It's like a sixth sense and needs to be heeded. I first experienced it while following those deer. It was eerie. I stopped and slowly turned around. A little spike buck had circled behind me and stood about forty yards away. I released my safety and aimed right between his eyes. Those old military rifles weren't designed for accuracy. The bullet knocked off his left antler. That was the first and only time I've tried a head shot. He turned to run as I jacked in a second shell and shot him through the ribs.

There I was, all alone. I had watched my dad field dress a couple deer, but I had never gutted one myself. Of course I managed to cut into the stomach and make quite a mess of things right off the bat. I pulled out the stomach and intestines, then split up through the ribs and removed the lungs and heart. I had seen my dad carry an animal across his shoulders. I tried to do likewise but couldn't get under it. So I removed the head and draped the carcass around my back, pulling the front legs over my shoulders. I'll never do that again. With that little white tail flapping behind, it's a good way to get shot. Good thing it was dark.

I had no idea where I was. The moon and a few stars gave little light and there was no evidence of a trail. I had sense enough to know that I had been walking downhill and needed to reverse. I also knew that the cabin should be somewhere off to my left. In the distance I heard a motor chugging away and used it as a bearing. Thankfully, it was the generator at our cabin. I stumbled through the trees and brush for more than an hour before banging on the cabin door. There I stood, covered in blood from head to toe. Jack the Ripper couldn't have been scarier looking. My dad made a big deal out of it. I was the only hunter of the group to fill his tag.

"WATCH ME BLOW off your little toe." Jim was sitting at our kitchen table fiddling with his .30-30. I was standing at the stove frying bacon and eggs in celebration of shooting a little doe earlier in the morning. I flipped an egg and forced a laugh. I don't like people pointing a gun at me – loaded or unloaded. Some things aren't funny. All laughing ceased when fire and smoke erupted from the muzzle of the rifle. As the smoke cleared, my stomach was in my chest and my heart was in my throat. A small hole appeared where my foot had been a nanosecond earlier. Jim was peakish as a newt in a mud puddle. "I slipped," he said.

I met Jim in the little mill town of Valsetz, Oregon, located in the Coastal Range of Western Oregon. There's nothing there now, and there wasn't much then. I had gone there to live with my dad who was working in a plywood mill. Initially we lived in a bunkhouse where no food was allowed. The owner of the bunkhouse also owned the only store and restaurant, two gas pumps, and a two-lane bowling alley. Valsetz had a grade school and a small high school. All thirty-five students plus the teaching staff could ride in one bus. That year it rained, not twelve inches, but twelve *feet* of water. As a teenager in Woodburn I wouldn't have been caught dead with an umbrella. In Valsetz you wouldn't be caught dead without one.

There was not a lot of entertainment for young people. Hunting and fishing was limited because of the rain and jungle-like growth of the coastal forest. Jim was my best friend and by default became my only hunting buddy. He had a couple old guns he had inherited from his grandpa. Come duck season I talked him into hiking to a pond where we occasionally fished for bass. I nearly had a heart attack when Jim's shotgun fired from behind me. A limb above my head disappeared. Leaves and twigs sprinkled onto my hat and shoulders. I slowly turned. "What was that?"

Jim's eyes darted back and forth. "I th-th-thought the s-s-safety was on."

"You tried out the safety with your shotgun pointed toward my head? You idiot! Why do you even have a shell in the chamber?" I glared at Jim and Jim stared at a tree for a couple minutes while my long life of fifteen years flitted before my eyes.

"Tell you what," I said. "You go first."

If there were ducks there before, that blast ended any chance finding them. We stood on the shore forlornly looking across a dismally vacant pool of water.

"Jim," I asked. "Do you mind if I try out your shotgun? I've never shot a 12-gauge."

His shotgun was a single shot, feather light with a straight stock. It didn't have a recoil pad, just a hard metal butt plate. I was about to shoot at a stump when a lone duck swooped across the pond. I turned and fired. The blast sat me down! The bruise on my shoulder lasted the next two weeks. The duck splashed into the water about twenty-five yards from shore. There was no boat. We didn't have a fishing line or piece of rope to throw over it. A tree limb wouldn't reach. *What were we thinking?*

My dad taught me that a true sportsman always retrieves what he shoots, and that he never shoots what he won't eat. I stripped down to my undies and walked as far as possible down a short log that lay in the water. Lily pads nestled on the surface, so I figured the water couldn't be very deep. I stepped off the log and...yikes! I found myself flailing in water that was over six feet deep. It's a good thing I can swim. I was shivering and breaking into goose bumps by the time I paddled back with the duck.

One other thing about Jim's 12-gauge. You could see small ripples in the barrel where it was warped to the left. That seemed pretty cool to me. As long a bird was flying from right to left, there was no need to take a lead. Just aim and shoot. A gun like that probably should have been retired.

The first panic attack I've experienced happened while hunting with Jim. The woods around Valsetz were so dense that you needed at least two hunters to get a deer. The idea is similar to having a beater and a shooter. The animal moves away from one person and into the sights of the other. We had come along tracks crossing a logging road, so I hiked into the trees about twenty yards, intending to "beat" the bush parallel to the road. Jim slowly commenced down the track watching for a deer to cross. I slipped through the brush expecting to hear a shot any second.

As the sun set and dusk crept through the trees I cut back toward the road and walked and walked and walked. The road had disappeared. It was like waking up in a scary movie. I sat on a fallen tree not knowing what to do. When a squirrel snapped a twig I envisioned a cougar creeping up behind me. Then I remembered the bears we'd seen at the local dump. What if a hungry bear was scouring the woods for its next meal? Suddenly an animal came crashing through the brush. I took off running. Branches and nettles scratched my face. Fallen limbs bruised my shins. I tripped and fell, jumped up and ran some more. A limb caught me across the chest and clotheslined me onto my back. I lay on the ground struggling to breathe. An inner voice whispered, *Calm down. You've got a gun that will bring down a bear. Get a grip.*

I struggled to my feet and picked up my rifle, then sat on a log. Dad's last words that morning as he headed to the mill were, "If you're not back shortly after dark, I'll have my whole shift out looking for you, so don't get lost." What would my friends think? I would never survive the embarrassment. In the distance I heard the *kwhump, kwhump* of the pumping station at the plywood mill. Problem solved. Just follow the sound. Guess what I found after twenty minutes of thrashing through ferns and trees? The road. It had taken a right angle turn shortly after I entered the brush. Jim had followed the road east as I continued south. Once it got dark, he went home, thinking I had left him. Some hunting pal he was! *Lesson to self:*

before hunting an area, check the general layout on a map and always carry a compass.

CITY SLICKERS

DAD AND I moved back to Idaho when I was sixteen. My new buddy, Mike, loved to talk about guns and hunting. He had his dad's Springfield .30-06, and I had my Lee Enfield. We also had .22 pistols. Mine was a Ruger Bearcat and Mike owned a Colt Frontier Scout. Idaho allowed open carry and we sometimes strapped on our pistols and headed for the hills to shoot rabbits. I don't remember seeing any bunnies, but we shot dozens of cans. Dressed in our western boots and hats we felt like real cowboys. We wouldn't dream of hunting without our six-shooters. I mean, what if you came across a rattlesnake or needed a final kill shot for a deer? Or more important, what if some outlaw tried to rob you?

I don't recall that Mike and I ever actually shot anything. I suspect it was our own fault. For example: duck hunting. We arrived at a duck pond one morning well before daylight. Ducks were quacking and feeding.

We sat in the car talking about girls and telling jokes when we should have been sneaking into a good position beside the slough. By half an hour before sunrise there wasn't a duck within five miles. We'd been having such a good time that we didn't even hear them leave.

Years later I heard an allegory which has greatly improved my hunting: *A leaf fell to the ground in the woods: the deer heard it; the bear smelled it; and the eagle saw it.* So, first rule: Be quiet. Animals have a good sense of hearing. Second rule: Stay downwind from your prey. Human beings have a definite smell, some much worse than others. Third rule: blend in. So far as I know, most animals are colorblind, but there's no missing a shape that doesn't belong in the surroundings.

Our first deer hunt was a disaster. We planned to camp but forgot the tent, the sleeping bags, and the dishes. Spending the night in the car wasn't so bad but drinking coffee from a rusty tin can found along the road and eating fried eggs and bacon off a moldy old rock with your fingers is not a great way to start the day.

Our next foray was into the snow-covered mountains of central Idaho. A tent, sleeping bags, and axe were stuffed in the trunk of my '57 Ford Fairlane; plenty of grub and camp dishes filled two coolers placed in the back seat; and a toboggan was strapped to the top of the car. We meant business.

We drove to Idaho City about forty miles northeast of Boise and had breakfast at a small diner, then struck north into the Boise National Forest. Around 11:00 we stopped at an isolated clapboard shed, aka store. I swaggered in with my cowboy hat and six shooter. Mike followed. We must have looked like a couple of real city slickers. A weathered old lady eyed us from behind the till. She wore bib overalls and a tattered olive-green work shirt. Straggly grey hair stuck straight out from a John Deer hat. Her black eyes and a large wart on a beaked nose reminded me of the old woman in *Hansel and Gretel.* I couldn't help glancing around to see if there was a big oven in the room. Rather than offering us gingerbread cookies, she reached under the counter and pulled out a Smith and Wesson 357. My knees began to shake. If she was expecting trouble, she wouldn't get any from us. We bought two cokes and made a quick exit.

By one o'clock we were plowing through snow and ice on an abandoned logging road. The grade got steeper and steeper as the snow got deeper and deeper. As long as we were going uphill I felt confident to continue. The Ford finally high centered and even with chains would go no further. So we loaded the toboggan and grunted another mile to a suitable campsite.

We cleared an area and started a fire. Then Mike scouted for more wood while I erected the tent.

"Ow, OWW, OWWW!"

I dropped a tent pole and ran toward the scream. "Where are you? What is it?"
Mike was doubled up on the ground holding his knee. The axe lay in a pool of blood.

"I chopped my knee. OWWW."

I quickly cinched an old blue bandanna around his leg. Mike put one arm around my neck, and we hobbled back to camp. *O God,* I prayed. *How am I going to get him back to town? O God, what am I going to do?* I propped him beside the fire where he sat staring into the flames. Giant snowflakes settled on the roof of our tent. The tracks from the toboggan slowly disappeared beneath a blanket of white. I had to decide whether to make several trips with the sled or just get Mike out. A coyote howled in the darkness and its pack chorused a reply. No way would I leave the safety of the fire for the uncertainty of the dark. I decided to doctor Mike the best I could and wait till morning.

As if in answer to my prayer, a Jeep Gladiator rumbled up and stopped beside the tent. Two men stepped out. Both wore army camo pants, thick quilted coats, and heavy red flannel hunting caps.

"Howdy," said the burlier of the two. He glanced around our camp and then, along with his buddy, squatted beside the fire. "What's up with your friend?"

"While he was chopping a limb from a tree, the axe slipped and caught him in the knee. I got him back to camp but we need help. I don't think I can get him off the mountain by myself."

The smaller fellow immediately went to Mike, laid him in a prone position and raised his legs.

"You don't know much about first aid, do ya?" he said. "Can't ya tell that your friend is in shock? I just got out of the Navy as a medic, and this boy needs some serious attention. It looks like he's lost a lot of blood. Let me look at that wound. And by the way, my name's Les, and that's Fred."

He removed the faded bandanna and cut Mike's pant leg from ankle to mid-hip. A deep slice into the leg leered like the grin of a vampire in a scary movie. Dark purple blood quickly covered the white bone of Mike's knee.

Les pressed the scarf into the wound and looked at me. "You had that bound so tight he could have lost his leg. Keep the pressure on this while I get my first-aid kit. Six or seven stitches will seal it nicely. I've seen much worse and can stitch it right now. You're darn lucky we came around."

Mike was woozy and confused, but he knew a needle when he saw one.

"What are you doing?" he slurred.

"Good. You're comin' around," replied Les. We'll have ya fixed up in no time."

"Are you a doctor?"

"No, but I was a Navy medic in Nam. Just relax. Here's a few pain killers to help ya get through this."

"Get through this? You're not going to touch me. I want to see a doctor!"

"Look. There ain't no doctor within a hundred miles. Anything a doctor can do, I can do. Then your buddy can get you off this mountain."

Mike rolled away from Les and tried to scramble to his feet. "Get your hands off me!"

Fred and I pinned him to the ground.

His eyes bulged, and his speech slurred. "Get away from me! I want a doctor."

Les again stuffed the wound with the bloody bandanna. "Alright, alright," he said. "No needles. But at least let me disinfect it and put a butterfly bandage on it. If your buddy has to put a tourniquet on that leg, you could lose it."

Forty-five minutes later Mike was sleeping beside the fire. His leg was wrapped in gauze and propped on a log. By this time Les and Fred realized that the Ford they had passed a mile back was mine. We discussed my plight. Their camp was further up the mountain. They promised to come back the following morning to cart Mike and all our gear back to my car. Sometimes I wonder if they weren't a couple of those angels mentioned in the Bible.

Three days later Mike limped into the office of what he considered to be a "real" doctor. The wound had begun to knit together but the old sawbones insisted on opening it to ensure it had been properly cleaned. Personally, I would have had it stitched by the medic. There was no question about stitches this time. When the doctor finished, he said, "Whoever treated you, did a perfect job. I couldn't have done better. If we hadn't torn it open, you wouldn't have needed stitches. Come back in a couple weeks and I'll pull these out."

I GRADUATED FROM high school the following spring and took a summer job in a small sawmill near Stanley, Idaho. It was a sad operation. Five men lived in a dilapidated, vermin infested camp. I shared a large bed with the hairiest guy I'd ever met. It wouldn't have been so bad if the fellow hadn't tossed and turned all night. Even with one arm draped over the edge of the bed I couldn't maintain enough distance to keep his furry legs from brushing against me. To top that, the sound of mice running up and down the walls and across the floor was a definite hindrance to getting any sleep. Ted, that was the guy's name, told me that sometimes mice ran across the top of the sheets at night. He said that one night he woke to see a rat jump onto the bed and scare off a mouse that was chewing on the blanket. The second night I slept in the back of the '56 Chevy pickup I had traded for earlier in the spring. An old army cot and my sleeping bag weren't very comfortable, but I felt much safer on several levels.

The crew had a problem. No paychecks had been issued for over a month. Therefore no one had paid their board. The cookie, wife of a sawyer named Jim Wakefield, was stressed to the max trying to feed everyone. She was the only woman in camp and not delighted about cooking in the first place. I had been raised to pull my own weight but had spent my last five bucks for gas on the way to the camp. I began praying, *give us this day our daily bread,* with new fervor. I prayed for the cook and prayed for our boss and prayed for the crew. More specifically, I prayed for a way I could personally help. The answer came in the form of a beat-up Lee Enfield I found in the back of the bunkhouse closet. I just "happened" to have five .303 shells in the jockey box of the Chevy. If five stones were sufficient for David to take on Goliath, five bullets should be plenty for me.

At breakfast the following morning I announced that I was going to shoot a deer for the crew.

Jim shook his head and laughed. "You're crazy. With all the racket we make, there isn't a deer within ten miles of here." He looked around the table. "When's the last time any of you boys saw a deer anywhere near?" Everyone was giving me the *look at that dumb, scrawny little eighteen-year-old* grin. I heard a couple snickers from the other end of the table.

Josh Jinkins, the fellow who pulled green chain, winked at Jim and asked me, "Ya gonna rope the danged thing, hit it with a rock, or club it with a board?"

"No," I said. "I found a .303 in the back of the bunkhouse and I have ammo for it."

"That old thing hasn't seen a cleaning rod in ten years. What makes ya think it'll hit anything?"

I hadn't thought about the condition of the rifle. I had nothing to clean it with and not enough bullets to take a test shot but getting a deer was now a matter of personal pride.

At the end of the day I pocketed my bullets, slung the rifle on my shoulder, marched down the road, and turned into the woods. A trail led through the trees up a hillock that flanked the east side of the camp. About three quarters of a mile up the slope a small four-point buck nibbled away at a patch of ragweed. It kept eating as I emerged from the trees. One shot and it was mine. I gutted it and proceeded to drag the carcass down the hill. A deer slides easy enough as long as you pull with the lay of the fur. When I came to the road I left the animal and hiked back to camp.

Josh Jinkins was sitting on the porch of his cabin enjoying a cigarette as I approached. "Aha," he laughed. "Here comes the great white hunter. Did ya run out of rocks or what?" Then he noticed the blood stains on my jeans. "Well I'll be jiggered! Ya actually got one."

"Hey fellas," he shouted. "We got ourselves a hunter!"

The crew gathered around as I told my story. Considering there was no television and only one radio, I was the best entertainment they'd had all week. Josh and Jim joined me to hike back to the buck. Within an hour the deer was hung, skinned, and Jim was slicing steaks and roasts. The following morning Mrs. Wakefield cooked up venison chops and smothered them with thick, creamy gravy. We were a happy crew that day. Within three days the meat was totally consumed but that was long enough for paychecks to arrive and for the Wakefields to make a trip to Stanley for supplies.

A little lesson in faith that I've learned. I'm not certain my prayers move God one way or the other. I do know that my prayers move me. When I act on them, the answers seem to come. I'm reminded of the apostle Peter's concern about paying taxes. Jesus sent him fishing and God provided. Seems to me that authentic faith is not what a guy believes but what he does.

Going into the third week, my dad drove in to see how I was doing. He was moving from Idaho to Oregon and happened to bring along a large Siamese cat named Sam. We put Sam in the mouse infested cabin for the night. The following morning the feline was flopped out on the floor, his belly bulging, and a tail hanging from his mouth. He could barely move. Bits and pieces of sixteen mice littered the corners of the shack. Sam was the kind of hunter I don't care for. He'd stuff himself and keep on killing just for fun. According to Ted, only the gentle pad of paws were heard the second night as Sam patrolled his new domain.

Dad was shocked at conditions in the camp, especially the lack of safety. There were no guardrails along the narrow ramps that flanked the massive sawblade. Chains and belts operated without safety shields. Can you imagine a sawyer making balance adjustments with his arms stretched as far as possible on either side of a running circular blade? My dad was convinced there would be a serious accident before the end of the season and urged me to come with him to Oregon. I talked with my boss. I still hadn't received my first paycheck and he decided to lower my wage from two dollars an hour to a buck fifty. He insisted that he wasn't getting his money's worth out of me and that I shouldn't expect more than a "training" wage. He promised he'd put my check in the mail at the end of the month. That was the summer of 1968 and I'm still waiting.

FIVE YEARS PASSED before I again picked up my Lee Enfield. In the meantime, working on a ranch while attending college in the piney woods of East Texas introduced me to water moccasins, copperheads, and rattlesnakes. I've stories to tell, but the snakes were doing the hunting and I was doing the hiding. I hate those things, especially the copperheads. Those critters don't give warning. They just lay coiled up on the trail and wait for you to step on them. Water moccasins proliferated the banks along the swamps where we ran fences. Once I was thrown by a horse while crossing a bog. Darn if a big cottonmouth didn't swim out and circle me. Rattlesnakes were not as common. The one that I remember was scooped up by a hay baler and mad as hades when it came out where I was stacking bales. That's the closest I've come to being struck. Puff adders weren't deadly unless you had a weak heart. You'd nearly wet yourself when one unexpectedly reared its head from the grass, spread its neck like a cobra, and had a hissy fit.

A few students had handguns. After all, it was Texas. I recall the guys taking the front-end loader to a spot where a culvert ran under the road between two sloughs. They'd drop the bucket above the culvert and shoot at the cottonmouths fleeing from both ends. I'm not one for that kind of "hunting." On the other hand, you don't want a nest of water moccasins too close to the swimming hole. Looking back I'm surprised at how much swimming I did while in Texas. Just the thought of a snake or a leech will get me out of the water faster than a cat can bat a mouse.

My junior and senior years were spent in Southern California. I'm ashamed to admit that I didn't take the opportunity to fish or hunt in California. Study and work took all my time. *What was I thinking?*

ALLIGATORS OF THE NORTH

PRINCE ALBERT, SASKATCHEWAN was my first pastoral assignment. It is uniquely situated for fishing and hunting. The prairies fan out to the south, offering a plethora of geese and ducks. Rolling hills, forests, and the Canadian Shield sweep to the north. It's a land of moose and deer, pike and walleye, geese and ducks.

The downside of the North is the black flies, mosquitoes, deer flies, no-see-ums, and other mini monsters whose sole purpose is to keep sportsmen out of the wilderness. How bad? Park your truck in the woods and you'll think you've stopped in the middle of a logging operation. The buzz and drone of the little blood-sucking critters will drive you bats. Roll up the windows and close the vents. Royal Army Sappers couldn't be more intent on getting through. How bad? So bad that bush pilots will not leave their planes after a crash. To do so invites insanity within a couple days. In summer the moose run themselves ragged trying to escape the little beasts. There's a reason moose stay in the water and near the bogs. I'm convinced that bug repellant came about through divine revelation.

Northern pike, affectionately known as jackfish, are one of my favorites. The first time I landed a pike I was sitting opposite my wife, Lin, in a canoe fishing for perch. The fishing map showed that particular lake as "fished out." The water was calm, and the sun was shining. A small zephyr kept the bugs away. It was an idyllic day for relaxing on the water. Fishing is not always about catching. It's about being there. But joy of joy, I was pulling out one perch after another. The same could not be said on Lin's end of the canoe. I can't understand how two people can be in the same boat with the same poles, the same reels, using the same bait, and one catches all the fish. It was important to me that she get "hooked" on fishing. So even though our fishing gear was identical, we traded poles. I kept landing little perch. Then we swapped seats, not an easy maneuver in a small canoe. I quickly reeled in three more.

Then my line snagged. I pulled hard but instead of the line breaking, something budged at the bottom of the lake. I figured it was an old log. Then the "log" began to slowly pull the canoe through the water. What the...? I pulled. It pulled. A guy has to be careful fishing with eight-pound test line on a ten-dollar pole. After thirty minutes, a thirty-seven-inch northern pike surfaced alongside the canoe. It was like bringing up a prehistoric monster. The average length for pike is only twenty-two inches. The record is around fifty-nine. The obvious problem was how to get it into the canoe. I whacked it with a canoe paddle, then managed to hook my fingers into the gills and pull it aboard.

Forty-five minutes later I played a second pike to the surface. *Snap!* It broke the line with a simple flick of the tale. A half hour later, a third humungous fish lay stretched on the water beside the canoe. It dove, cutting the line with the most wicked set of teeth I'd ever seen. Not to be outdone, we paddled to shore and drove to town. I bought a large net and sped back to the lake. By sunset a second jackfish lay on the bottom of the canoe.

The pike is an aggressive fish that you can probably catch using a bottle opener for a lure. How aggressive? It will eat other jackfish when food is scarce. It has a snout-like mouth with hundreds of teeth, some needle-like, and others like fangs. Their snouts remind me of alligators. Yep, probably the closest thing you can find to an alligator in Canada. After those first two, I bought a jaw spreader to hold those powerful snouts open and an Eagle Claw hook remover for reaching in. No point in losing a finger. Some fishermen refuse to land a pike into their boats because the fish exudes a snotty-like mucus while flopping around. But for the guy who takes one home, large fillets of mild, white flesh await.

A NEIGHBOR TOLD me about a pond north of Prince Albert that was "loaded" with perch. Lin was "perched out" but I'm not averse to an afternoon by myself. I dug a can of worms, packed my rod and reel, and loaded the canoe atop our Chevy. Within forty-five minutes I was parked beside a delightful pond surrounded by rolling fields of wheat. A couple meadow larks sang greetings to me. Red-winged black birds flitted back and forth through a cluster of cattails. With the warm sunshine and a slight breeze, everything was perfect. Well, not quite everything. The breeze kept the mosquitoes away, but it kept blowing the canoe past a weed bed where the fish were feeding. On my third pass I had one of those strikes that keep you awake at night. A perch (or pickerel or whatever) attacked my hook and charged toward the middle of the pond. As the line stripped from the reel, I locked the drag. *Snap!* Hook, line, and sinker – gone! *Lesson to self: Let a fish run and then work it to the boat. Also, make certain the drag is properly set.*

More whoppers might be lurking in the same hole, but I needed an anchor to hold the canoe in place. So back to shore I paddled. I had a roll of nylon rope. A rock secured to the end would be just the thing. Do you think I could find one? I searched the shoreline. I walked the road fifty yards in both directions. There was hardly a pebble let alone anything resembling a rock. I rummaged through the trunk of the car. Aha! The mini-spare. There was a slim chance I might lose it, but I'd have to risk it. Fishing is important. I tied the spare to the end of the rope, then doubled the knot. Returning to the weed bed, I tossed the wheel into the pond. Boy oh boy! Two seconds later the spare bobbed to the surface as the wind blew canoe *and* anchor toward the shore. What the...? I quickly looked around to see if anyone was watching, pulled the tire into the canoe, and paddled back to the car. No fish were coming home that day.

THERE'S A STRING of lakes and portages for canoeists in Prince Albert National Park. Our favorite day trip was a visit to Grey Owl's cabin on the shore of Kingsmere Lake. He and his wife, Anahereo, had lived there with a family of beavers. Sounds gross, but it couldn't be any worse than a house full of cats or dogs. Grey Owl was an influential conservationist in the 1930s. His real name was Archibald Stansfeld Belaney. I can't blame him for changing it. Only problem, he claimed to be half Apache from the southern United States, and people don't take kindly to a liar.

Our oldest son, Mike, was introduced to fishing at the park. He was only eighteen months old at the time and I had equipped our canoe for playtime and naptime. We were paddling on one of the Hanging Heart Lakes when I cast into a weed bed. *Wham!* I hooked a real fighter. Mike was hanging over the gunnel, fascinated by a long, speckled jackfish. The fish became quite docile once reaching the surface but went berserk when I dropped it from the net into the canoe. *Flop, wiggle, whap, thump!* Little Mike fled from my end of the canoe to his mother's arms. A crowbar wouldn't have pried him loose. That's a poor way to introduce a little boy to fishing!

My dad and stepmother, Lois, drove all the way from Portland, Oregon to see us. I insisted on taking them to the Prince Albert National Park for a "cruise" around Lake Waskesiu. Our twelve-foot rental boat with a ten-horse outboard was maxed to capacity when loaded with four adults, a baby, and a miniature Schnauzer. That wouldn't have been a problem if it hadn't been for the storm. I don't mean a gentle breeze accompanied by a slight drizzle. I'm talking a Texas toad strangler with black angry clouds, thunder and lightning, and gale-force wind. We were caught in the middle of the lake. The shore was lined with trees and rocks and there was no place to beach the boat. Had we tried, the craft would have foundered and capsized. The only choice was to run with the wind. The outboard at full throttle couldn't keep up with the waves surging past. The stern fishtailed in a vain effort to push us to safety. Swells rose and fell like waves on the ocean. Up, up, up; down, down, down. *Thump!* The keel struck the bottom of the lake. Then, up, up, up; down, down, down. *Thump!*

A large rescue craft appeared through the rain and mist. Thank God the rental office informed park rangers of a missing party. Search and rescue had failed to locate anyone along the shores and feared the worst. We passed up our toddler and then Lois, followed by my wife, my dad, and Salty, our Schnauzer. I handed the tiller to a muscled park warden in a wet suit. My stepmother vowed she would never again get into anything smaller than a cruise ship.

THE FOLLOWING SUMMER a neighbor named Craig asked if I'd be interested in canoeing into a restricted lake for three days of pike and pickerel fishing. It was like asking if the Pope was a Catholic. I'm talking forty years ago, so some details are sketchy. I'll just say it was Lake Mantepsepou, a Greek word for "guess where?" As I recall, the lake was off limits to float planes; there was no road going in; and no motorized boats were allowed. The only access was by canoe, which meant a full day of paddling up a medium size creek. Much of the time was spent dragging Craig's old green canoe up shallow stream beds and hefting it over one beaver dam after another. I must have gone through a full jug of Muskol bug repellant in a vain effort to fight off mosquitoes and black flies.

After seven hours of sweat, colorful language, and a thousand bug bites, we portaged around a beaver dam into a pristine lake snuggled between two hills in the treed wilderness of Northern Saskatchewan. An easy thirty minutes of paddling landed us on a sandy peninsula near a freshwater spring. We quickly pitched the tent and secured our gear. Supper could wait. We were there to fish.

I've never seen fish hit like those fish. Every cast, well maybe two out of three, hooked either a pike or a pickerel. If ever there was a fisherman's heaven, Mantepsepou Lake was the place. By evening Craig and I landed at least a hundred fish between us. I know you think I'm exaggerating but our biggest problem was which fish to keep. The regulations allowed an aggregate possession of ten fish. Here's the dilemma: when you have two days to fish, how can you know if the next cast won't hook an even bigger fish than the one before? And do you want to keep large pike or go with walleyes which are much better eating? We clipped the barbs off our hooks to make for quicker catch and release and kept a couple walleyes for supper. The plan was to fill the cooler the following day.

Saskatchewan surely has the most beautiful skies in the world. Seemingly every star in the universe twinkled down that night. The northern lights danced with yellow and pink and purple swirls. The gentle lap of water on the beach was accented with the forlorn call of a loon. Craig and I settled back on our elbows and savored the moment. "Oh Canada, our home and native land!"

Time came to secure the zippers and screens on the tent, light a mosquito coil, and roll out our sleeping bags.

"Good night, Craig. I sure appreciate you inviting me on this trip," I said as I adjusted my pillow. The only reply was the muffled snore of a man lost in dreams of rods and reels.

Whup-whup-whup-whup. "What the...? Where am I?" One moment I was dreaming of beaver dams and the next moment my eyes opened to the sound of a helicopter. "What the...?" The tent was filled with smoke. Craig was coughing in his sleep.

"Craig! Wake up! There's a fire."

We tumbled out into a world of ash and smoke. The sides of the tent fluttered in a stiff breeze. Lake Mantepsepou lay hidden in a deep, murky haze. The drone of an aircraft, most likely a water bomber, passed overhead. Within minutes our gear was piled into the canoe and we were on the water. What to do? We had no way of knowing the direction of the fire or how close we were to the blaze. The plane flew west, so we paddled east toward the outflow where we had entered the lake.

It was a tough paddle, taking us directly into the wind. Waves broke over the bow. I could barely see through my glasses. Our gear was waterlogged. Water pooled around my knees. We couldn't stop to bail without being blown back where we had come from, or worse, losing our track and flipping the canoe. I only knew to paddle and paddle hard. A crossing that had taken thirty minutes the day before, took an hour and a half before we entered the creek. What a relief to be surrounded by spruce and jack pine. Leaves trembled and waved to us from the occasional aspen. Gradually the smoke cleared. Even with the shallows and beaver dams, the trip going downstream was a dream. And the fish box? Empty, of course. *Lesson to self: always keep the first few fish.*

WINTERS ARE LONG and cold in Saskatchewan. I decided Lin needed a surprise and secretly booked a trip to Honolulu. I arranged a stay with the grandparents for Michael, our little boy, purchased airline tickets, and booked the hotel. I insisted we take only our swimsuits and two empty suitcases. We would purchase anything we needed when we reached our destination. She was still in suspense as we arrived at the airport. Oh the smile in her Irish eyes as we boarded a plane bound for Hawaii.

Canadians, at least those from Saskatchewan, are easy to identify in Hawaii. The first time I entered the elevator in our hotel I was surrounded by men wearing blue and white flowered beach shirts that were identical to mine. The Sears mail-order catalogue was quite popular in the prairies. And you immediately recognize Canuks who have just arrived. Fish belly white skin of the northern clime turns to lobster red the first day on the beach.

Technically this was not a fishing expedition but being surrounded by sixty million square miles of ocean made it impossible not to give fishing some serious thought. Over three hundred varieties of fish lurk in Hawaiian waters. Those fit for home cuisine are displayed on table after table at the fish market. My reel fingers twitched in envy as I viewed salmon, tuna, swordfish, and snapper laid on ice. Lobster and prawns were in abundance. Scallops, clams, and oysters teased my palate. Octopus and squid spread their tentacles for those with exotic tastes. I secretly dreamt of getting certified for scuba diving and imagined the thrill of spearing a grouper or a giant bluefin. Taking Lin on an amorous dinner cruise versus booking an exclusive fishing charter taxed my love to the limit, but a man does what a man has to do. It was "Tiny Bubbles" time. That was more than forty years ago, and we've now passed fifty years of marital bliss.

The closest I came to fishing was an afternoon of snorkeling at Hanauma Bay. Imagine turquoise water that turns to translucent emerald as it rolls toward silver sand and scattered palms. A ridge of reef protects this idyllic bay from the restless waters of the Pacific. Hawaiian snorkeling is like swimming in a gigantic aquarium of tropical fish – pinks and yellows, reds and purples, striped and speckled.

Our guide informed us that larger, more spectacular creatures could be seen on the ocean side of the reef. "However," he warned, "those waters are only for the most experienced swimmers." Surely he was talking about me. I've been on swim and water polo teams. I took a competitive diving class – that was a belly flop.

Within minutes I walked across the top surface of the reef and leapt into the deep. Suddenly protection from the currents and waves was gone. *What was I thinking?* Waves hammered me against a sharp wall of coral embedded rock. I cut my palms and fingers in a vain effort to climb to safety. A drowned victim with shredded hands and knees crossed my imagination. I floundered with great windmill strokes to escape the force of the tide. Then came panic and hyperventilation. I sucked salt water through the snorkel and began to choke. An inner voice whispered, *if you don't' calm down, you're going to drown.* The rise and fall of the tide pulling me out to sea was terrifying. I finally managed to get a grip. I'm a strong swimmer and with the fins and snorkel could stay afloat a long time, but would it be long enough? How soon would I be missed? When would a search be organized? And then...*O God if you just get me out of this one.*

Far below me I noticed two scuba divers exploring the ocean floor. I motioned for help, but they didn't see me. They had come from somewhere, and they had to surface sometime. Wherever they swam on the bottom, I swam on the surface. After what seemed like an eternity they came to a channel in the reef. I share this because it was the second time I've had a panic attack in the wilds and temporarily lost my mind; and it could have cost me my life. I've been to places where men have been swept off the rocks by rogue waves. I've read reports of fishermen who drowned because they didn't wear their life jackets. Hunters have frozen to death because they left their stalled vehicles during storms.

Lesson to self: listen to the guide, keep the rules, and error of the side of safety.

Little Mike trying out his first pole while visiting friends in Big River, Saskatchewan

BEATING THE BUSH

GETTING YOUR SIGHTS on a white tail in relatively flat, heavily forested land is a team effort. Eight years in northern Saskatchewan and I only twice took a bead on a deer without the help of at least one other person. We usually hunted in groups of three or four. My first hunt in Saskatchewan was with a party of five led by an old Métis by the name of Charlie Bruneau. Charlie was a bandy-legged trapper about sixty years old. He was a bit near-sighted and carried an old lever action Winchester .30-30 with open sights. He figured if he got close enough to see anything, a scope would be of no use.

Charlie positioned our group along a cutline that separated the deep woods from a block of timber where white tail deer were known to rest during the day. His two sons, Paul and Claude, a French fellow named Roger, and I waited as Charlie worked his way back and forth through the trees.

Whitetails are smart. You can be surrounded by them and never know it. I read that on average it takes twenty-five hours to see a white tail buck and a hundred hours to actually shoot one. Fortunately, Saskatchewan had an open season for does, because in eight years of hunting in Prince Albert I only recall seeing two bucks.

We waited and waited for Charlie to appear. I was beginning to doze when, *Thwack! Thwack! Thwack!* Charlie was smacking a log with a limb about twenty yards from the cutline. It was a double signal: first, to be ready; second, to let us know where he was when we started shooting.

Five seconds later, a large doe stuck her head out of the trees and looked down the cut. Paul Bruneau, Charlie's youngest son, took a shot. He was a flighty guy that always "jumped the gun." Seven deer burst from the woods charging for the safety that lay behind us. Hunters began firing and the herd turned down the cutline. Something I've never done is shoot an animal in the rump. It's a sure way to ruin a massive amount of meat and release the bowel and stomach contents. But what do you do when your deer is running directly away from you? I leaned as far as I could to the left and aimed at the back of the rib cage. *Kapow!* Down it went, an instant kill. The bullet had gone under the skin along the ribs, come out, and hit the doe in the side of the head just behind the ear. I couldn't have made a better running shot in my dreams. It was definitely a fluke, but the fellows thought I was the best crack shot they'd ever met. And I wasn't about to let them know any different. That was the last animal I bagged with the old Enfield. The following year I traded it for a .270 Winchester with a scope. I can't say the new rifle performed any better in placing meat in the freezer.

Later that winter Charlie took it on himself to teach me how to hunt moose. Unfortunately he was not much of a talker and I'm a slow learner. Paul and I drove behind Charlie's old Chevy to a stretch of woods known for good forage. Occasionally we stopped to check for fresh tracks – out of the truck, into the truck. I was wearing thick, heavy wool socks inside a pair of heavy rubber boots. Whenever we got out, the snow packed into the cleats of the boots. When we got in, the truck heater partially melted the snow which soon froze into thin layers of ice. Gradually my boots became encased in frozen snow and my toes began to freeze. Charlie noticed I was suffering and offered me a pair of moccasins. They were beautifully hand stitched and beaded, double lined, and came to midcalf. I was dubious. My boots had a tougher lining and cleated soles, but Charlie insisted. Fortunately there was a fairly heavy snow on the ground because a moccasin has no sole and no heel. I could feel every rock and limb underfoot. Without heels I began to walk more on my toes and was soon exercising the entire foot. Within minutes my toes thawed out and my feet were warm and toasty. The blood was circulating in ways impossible with heavy boots. Keep in mind, it was close to twenty below zero. Anytime I stopped walking, my feet soon felt the cold. The moccasins helped create heat, but they didn't hold it like a well-insulated boot.

We arrived at the end of a bush road. Charlie told Paul and me to wait and disappeared into the trees.

After forty-five minutes of starting the truck for heat, then turning it off to save fuel, and repeating the process, I said to Paul, "Where did he go?"

"I don't know," he replied.

"What's he doing and why are we here?"

"I don't know."

"I say we go find a moose."

Paul started his Ford and off we drove. Ten minutes later Charlie returned to find no one waiting. He had circled a frozen marsh, counting all the tracks going in and all the tracks coming out. With more tracks going in than coming out...well, you do the math. Two moose were waiting for two would be hunters who were mindlessly driving around the bush. I've never forgotten that lesson in tracking and *patience.*

THERE ARE MANY things to be learned from old timers. One of the biggest, always think about how to get the animal out of the woods *before* you pull the trigger. Here are a few corollaries. If hunting from the road, hunt on the upside, never on the downside. Dragging an animal uphill for half a mile is a sure prescription for a hernia. Never shoot something on the opposite side of a river. Unless you have a boat, you'll never find that spot after you cross a bridge and hike through the brush. Never take a bad shot. A wounded animal can travel for miles, and a sportsman has an obligation to track it down. When dragging an animal out, do it portage style. Carry a portion fifty feet or so, set it down and go back for a second load. Carry the second load fifty feet or so past the first and set it down. Then return for the first and repeat the process.

By leapfrogging the loads you get a bit of rest time between. I learned that from a First Nations friend and have used it many times.

I learned another trick that I'll probably never use. An old trapper named Melvin lived northeast of Tobin Lake. It was a late Indian summer with hot days and cool nights. One day while preparing his trap lines, he spotted a large moose along the shore of the South Saskatchewan River. Without giving it a second thought, he raised his rifle and fired. Down went the moose. A good size moose is a chore for two men and can take several trips to haul out. For one man, several miles from a drivable road and a month away from enough snow for a sled, forget it. Instead of field dressing the animal, Melvin covered it with heavy brush and resumed his business. He had trails to cut and supplies to haul. Several days later the moose was ripening from the heat and as bloated as a Goodyear blimp. Melvin rolled the animal into the river and floated it downstream to the small community where he lived. I suspect it tasted a bit gamey, but he had winter meat for himself and his family. A man does what a man has to do.

IT ONLY TAKES ONE

HOW A PERSON can grow up in Alberta without picking up a fishing rod or shouldering a gun is beyond me. I guess if you live in Edmonton or Calgary there are other things to hold your interest. When Doug came along as an associate I took it as my personal duty to convert him to hunting. We came from vastly different backgrounds. While I had been learning to read a map, follow a compass, and explore the vast outdoors, Doug had been investing in helmets, headlamps, and harness for caving. I don't know that he had ever been down a cave, but he had pretty well mapped out the entire Edmonton sewage system. He claimed there was a lot of history to be learned below the city streets and some real interesting finds. I had my own ideas about what you find down there.

The first thing Doug did was purchase a beautiful Remington 7mm Magnum with a Leupold scope. He must have thought that the rifle makes the hunter. I come from a family where you make do with any gun that shoots. I took Doug to a spot along the Saskatchewan River to sight in his rifle. He went through a box of shells before he hit the target, and a second box before he hit the center. Until I purchased my .270 I had always hunted with open sites. Using a scope was new for me and I went through a box and a half of shells adjusting it. Most of my shots are between fifty and a hundred yards, hardly enough distance to need a scope or a flat shooting .270. Old timers have been using the little lever action .30-30 Winchester for years without a scope and doing fine. Besides, in the bush a scope makes a twig look like a sequoia. I can honestly say that the .270 did not make me a better hunter. I can also say that it kicked like a mule. My shoulder was black and blue by the time I shot a box of shells, and I developed a habit of flinching and pulling to the right every time I squeezed the trigger.

Doug and I took a couple days off and drove to the little town of Big River. I always wondered about the name. It's not "big" and I never noticed any river. I do recall a lake that looked somewhat like a river. We started our trip early on a Monday morning. About twenty miles down the road I asked Doug, "Did you pick up more ammunition?"

"No," he said. "I have plenty."

"So how many shells do you have?"

"Five."

"Five? That's all?"

He gave me the knowing nod all hunters perfect. "It only takes one."

I rolled my eyes. "I know it only takes one. The question is which one."

I knew the perfect spot to post Doug for his first deer. To get there required driving around a long, frozen lake. Until I moved to Saskatchewan, I hadn't experienced cold. Imagine going through an entire February with the temperature staying close to minus forty. Every morning the car seats are as hard as rock, and you're lucky if the vinyl dash doesn't split. Tires freeze flat on one side sitting in the driveway, and you drive down the road with a *thump, thump, thump* until they round out. By late November you can drive across some northern lakes. I wouldn't have chanced it if we hadn't come across a set of truck tracks turning off a bush road and going across the center of the lake. The shortcut would give us an extra forty-five minutes or more of hunting. My philosophy, "What one man can do, another man can do. You just follow his lead, or in this case, his tracks." So, that's what we did.

I was tapping on the steering wheel and Doug was nodding to the beat of *On the Road Again*. Visions of deer – past, present, and future – danced in my brain. What the...? My tapping turned to a terrified grip on the wheel as I slowed to a stop. Through the blowing snow the top half of a truck cab appeared above the surface of the ice. The driver's window was open, and footprints tracked across the snow going toward shore. I slowly reversed and gingerly turned around. I knew better than to sit there in shock and I also knew not to race for shore. A parked car is more likely to break through the ice than a moving vehicle, and a speeding car creates a pressure wave that can cause the ice to fracture. We opened the doors, prepared to bail out if necessary, and slowly idled our way back to shore. There's no more horrifying sound than the moan and quake of ice breaking up. *O God,* I prayed. *If you just get me out of this one.* By now you've probably figured out that that is my standard prayer for emergencies in the bush. God is probably beginning to wonder when I'll grow up. When we reached shore, I stopped the car. *Thank you Jesus!* It was fifteen minutes, a cup of coffee, and half a sandwich before my hands stopped shaking. I often wonder about the driver of that truck. We found where he had walked to shore, but his tracks ended at the road.

We drove to a spot where a small square of timber connects in one corner to the big woods. It was a trick I'd learned from Charlie Bruneau. Deer fed in the neighboring hay fields at night, moved into the timber block in the early morning, and then rested during the day. If disturbed, they took a trail to the corner that joined the big woods. I posted Doug at that corner. Guaranteed, I would drive some deer through, and he would get a shot. I then drove to the far end of the block and began to wend my way back and forth. There was about eighteen inches of snow and plenty of fresh tracks.

I didn't get far before nature called. There's two rules about doing a dump in the woods. Number one, keep your rifle within reach. The buck you've been following all morning is just waiting for you to squat with your trousers around your ankles before bounding out of the brush. Number two, it's better to take a wad of toilet paper in your back pocket than to trust any questionable leaves that might be handy. As luck would have it, I didn't have any toilet paper, and even "safe" foliage was not sufficient for my needs. So I cut off a swath of my shirt tail. When it's twenty below you don't take time for meditation; just get 'er done!

After about forty-five minutes I was getting close to Doug. Just when I thought we had missed the morning migration, BOOM! BOOM! BOOM! *That's three.* I was coming to an open fence line. BOOM! *That's four.* I wasn't about to leave the trees and cross that fence. It sounded like Doug was shooting at anything that moved. BOOM! *That's five.* I crawled through the fence and into the open.

Doug ran toward me yelling like a banshee, "It's still moving! It's still moving!"

We ran to the clearing where a blood trail led a large dry doe.

"Congratulations on your first deer, Doug. What was all that shooting about?" *Bet you wish you had picked up another box of shells. Hopefully, I'll get my deer this morning and you won't need them.* "Tell me what happened."

"I was sitting on that stump over there when four deer charged from those trees. They were running right at me. I didn't have time to aim so I started shooting from the hip." *Shots one, two, and three. This guy must have grown up with old episodes of Chuck Connors and The Rifleman.* "Three ran right past me. The other turned and ran down the fence line. I had time to aim and was sure I hit it." *Shot number four*. "I took my last shot as it ran over this knoll." *Shot number five!*

By noon I had tagged my deer. We field dressed both animals and parked in the middle of a frozen pasture enjoying a cup of coffee and rehearsing the morning's hunt. Can you believe this? I was biting into a peanut butter sandwich when a six-point buck wandered into the pasture and walked up to the car. It looked in the window, gave a snort, and then ambled into the trees. I was strongly tempted to drop him, drive back to town, and pick up another tag. *Only take what you need. And what you need is already dressed and tagged.*

Doug turned to me, "This is way too easy."

"Excuse me?"

"Next year I'm going bow hunting."

I recalled all the trails I had hiked, trees I had climbed, and toes I had frozen over the years. I generally put some meat in the freezer, but rarely was it as easy as Doug's first deer. But he was right about one thing, *it only takes one!*

DOUG PULLED A stunt the following year that bears mentioning. We were driving around the bend on a bush road and came on three deer browsing on wild roses about forty yards ahead. I stopped the truck and Doug climbed out with his rifle. The deer nibbled away showing no concern about our presence. This was about as easy as it gets. Doug raised his 7mm and fired. Deer scattered in three directions. Nothing fell.

The situation was such that I hadn't gotten out of the truck to back him up. Well, I got out then. "How in tarnation did you miss?"

"I don't know," he replied. "I raised my rifle and when the scope went black, I pulled the trigger."

"You mean you didn't aim?"

"I didn't think I needed to."

Don't tell anyone, but there are occasions that make this particular preacher cuss. Stupidity has to be a sin. We had a discussion in which I did all the talking. I told Doug about an elderly member of our congregation whose oldest son, Hank, was killed in a hunting accident. He and three buddies had seen a moose enter a thicket. A couple fellows were standing, and a couple were kneeling. One grunted through a birch bark megaphone, "ooommmah... ooommmah." Another peered through his scope at the brush. Hank stood up and *BANG!* He took a thirty-aught-six slug through the back of the head. When his dark hair had filled his buddy's scope, the man fired, thinking the moose had stepped out. I cannot preach enough about gun safety. Hunter safety courses should be required everywhere, maybe even a refresher course for old timers like myself. If you don't have any common sense, stay out of the bush.

I DIDN'T GIVE up on Doug. Everyone deserves a second chance. Truth be told, he was a willing learner, and I needed a partner for moose hunting.

We picked a patch of bush northwest of Prince Albert, packed our gear, and hit the road. The plan was to drive to a suitable area and camp for three days. We stopped at small pub for burgers and a beer on the way.

Part of hunting is having the right look. You quickly learn to swagger a bit and how to nod and wink. Vocabulary is important too. Knowing the difference between trailing and tracking, spotting and stalking, bulls and bucks, and cows and does is important in carrying on a conversation in a northern bar. After a few pints, terms like rut, grunt, snort, and rack, take on new meaning, but are important none the less. Knowing the difference between large caliber rifles can be a plus. Whenever I don't understand what is being said, I just give a wise nod and an "uh huh".

We were ordering from a stained and tattered menu when a big Ford F-150 pulled up. A fellow got out wearing bright yellow coveralls that had never seen a spot of blood or a spec of mud; probably hadn't been through their first wash. His shiny GOR-TEX boots had obviously never tromped through a puddle or a bog. This fellow could have been a model for Cabela's catalogue. He sat down at the bar and looked at an old timer named Rodney.

In a slow American drawl he said, "I'm just visitin' up here. Can ya tell me a good area to hunt for a buck moose?"

Rodney lowered his head and covered his mouth with his left hand doing his best not to snicker. He quickly gained control and answered, "As a matter of fact, I do. There's a moose crossing up the road about a mile and a half. You'll see the sign. Just pull over and park. Best to sit on the tailgate of your truck so you'll be ready. Moose cross the highway there all the time. Once you get your 'buck', come back and we'll give you a hand getting it into your truck."

"Thank ya kindly."

As the Ford pulled away, the entire pub roared with laughter. The bartender gave Rodney a pint "on the house" for the entertainment. Sitting on the tailgate of a truck for any length of time when it's minus twenty is sure torture – even worse than being bombarded by mosquitoes on a hot summer night while holding the bag for a snipe hunt. Then everyone began telling stories about American hunters.

"Did you hear the one about the guy from Ohio that shot a mule?" grinned Rodney. "When he came to a game check, the officer took a look and flagged him through. The officer's buddy said, 'Why didn't you ticket him?' He replied, 'If he's dumb enough to shoot the thing, he can darn well eat it.'"

To be fair, I lived in the United States for over twenty years. Hunters there tell the same stories about Canadians from cities like Vancouver and Toronto. Most hunting stories can easily be adjusted for either side of the border. I don't doubt that a few mules have been shot, but I'm not certain of their nationality.

Doug and I had just finished our burgers, and I was contemplating a big piece of lemon meringue pie and a cup of coffee when the F-150 roared into the parking lot and screeched to a stop. The door to the pub swung open and there stood the American with the biggest grin you ever saw. His new boots, one pant leg, and both hands were smeared with blood and hair.

"Thank ya'll," he said. "I never realized moose huntin' was so easy. I just sat there like ya said. It walked out of the woods and wham bam! Right beside the truck. Now what about that help ya'll promised?"

Well I never! When I think of all the driving I've done; of sitting for hours on cold mountain tops; of slogging through bogs; of wrecking my knees and ruining my boots; and not even seeing a track. Well I never!

DOUG AND I booked a room for the night and drove north early the next morning. We turned off the highway onto an old forestry road just as the sun was peaking from the east. Saskatchewan is pretty flat. Usually you need several buddies to walk through an area pushing deer or moose to hunters who are posted at clearings and crossings. Our chances were slim, but we had a fresh skiff of snow. This was a chance to practice what I'd learned from old Bruneau. I reminded Doug that we didn't want to hunt too far from the truck. Packing out several hundred pounds of meat is hard work, not that I would know.

We came across three sets of tracks leading into a large thicket of willows bordering a small marsh. I circled the area and determined that a bull, a cow, and a calf had entered the bog that morning. We were hoping to shoot the calf. Why? First, young calves don't usually survive a harsh winter. Second, hunting should be treated like cattle ranching. You don't shoot your breeding stock. Doug sat overlooking a low spot while I pushed through the willows and into the reeds. After the deer incident, he promised that if given another chance, he would take aim before shooting. I hadn't walked fifteen minutes when two shots rang out. I hustled back.

Doug's footprints led into the marsh. I found him surrounded by cattails beside a large splash of blood. I mentioned before that there is a difference between "trailing" and "tracking". Trailing is following a blood trail, whereas tracking is following footprints. The moose was badly wounded, and the blood trail was easy to follow but the tracks were those of a big bull, what old timers call a "baloney bull." Instead of tender steaks and roasts, we were chasing several hundred pounds of gamey tasting hamburger. That's probably why someone invented ketchup. We fought our way across the marsh and through the willows expecting any minute to see steam rising from a dark mound of muscle and brawn. But the trail went on and on and on. We tramped, then trudged further and further from the road. The trail passed from the marsh into an old clear cut. We labored over blow downs and into a swampy bog. About half a mile into the bog, we located the moose in a quagmire of dead trees and semi-frozen mud. I gutted him, but there's no way two church pastors whose chief form of exercise is tea and cookies with elderly parishioners are going to pack six or seven hundred pounds of moose out of a bog, across a clear cut, and through a marsh. We hiked to the truck, drove to the highway, and returned to the pub. Everyone agreed that only something like an amphibious ATV could reach that moose without sinking.

I told Doug that as bad as I felt about leaving the animal in the swamp, everything dies sometime. There would be some happy coyotes, wolves, or bears over the next few days. Rodney, perched at his regular barstool, was eavesdropping and interrupted.

"Horst can get that moose."

"Horst?"

"Yea, Horst Schmidt, a trapper lives other side of the bog. Got an old white mule name of Caspar. Horst will get your moose." He motioned to the waitress for a napkin and a pencil. "Finding his cabin can be tricky. I'll draw ya a map."

The following morning we drove up the highway, turned off on a decommissioned bush road, then into the woods on a dirt track. Soon brush and weeds scraped the bottom of the truck. Branches snagged the outside mirrors and scratched the sides. Horst lived off the grid and certainly didn't encourage visitors. But we were determined. They say the Lord helps those who help themselves. I've found that sometimes you have to pay for the help.

The road stopped at an ancient rusty Ford pickup. The windshield was smashed, the tires had rotted, and a scrubby little spruce was growing through the bed. Smoke ascending from a small hill marked the location of a cabin. I parked our truck, and we followed a path through the trees. A big white mule stood within what looked like a vintage collection of old prison bars formed from rusty bedposts, rails, and headboards. It was the strangest enclosure I ever saw. A bear could crawl over it; a deer could jump it; and a moose would just walk through it. Old pots and kettles hung here and there. Every one of them had a dark burn hole in the bottom from overheating on a woodstove. I guess Horst thought they'd make good alarms if anything crashed through the fence. A couple rusty worn-out Swede saws draped across a makeshift gate. The mule chewed on a stem of dry hay and gave me the evil eye. I don't think he took much to strangers.

The cabin was built from small logs chinked with moss and mud. A bear skin was nailed flesh side out beside the door. A couple blood-stained fleshing boards leaned against a fence rail.

I knocked, "Hello? Anybody home?"

A soft voice answered, "The door's open."

It was dark inside. A thin animal skin was stretched across the only window and was opaque at best. An oil lamp provided the only other light. The odor of rancid meat was powerful, and an indescribable aroma was drifting from a large pot atop an old potbelly stove. The heat and humidity rivaled a Finnish sauna.

"What do you want?" came a voice from the corner.

As my eyes adjusted, I saw an older woman propped up in a bed. A stack of fresh skinned beaver pelts, all on fleshing boards, leaned against the wall. There was fat and flesh on the bed covers and the floor. An oily feel was on everything. I soon figured out that Horst's wife was crippled, so he had set things up so she could flesh pelts without getting off the bed.

Before going further, I need to explain a few things about my partner. Doug was the fussiest guy I've known when it comes to health. He was a whole wheat, whole milk, fresh-squeezed juice junkie. He would drink a cup of coffee or tea only if it was the only way not to offend. Water was his drink of choice, followed by juiced carrots and other awful tasting vegetables. This is a serious handicap for a minister, country or urban. He always ate something just before we did visitations so he could politely decline coffee and cookies. Poor guy was teamed with me, an eight to ten cups of coffee a day, bacon and egg loving, fast food fiend.

We introduced ourselves and stated our mission. She said her name was Frieda and seemed mighty glad to see us. In fact, the poor woman was starved for conversation. I felt sorry for the old gal.

"Can I treat you men to a cup of tea?"

"No. No, ma'am," said Doug. "We're fine. We'll just sit and chat till your husband gets back."

Even with the crackling of wood in the stove and the bubbling of the pot, I heard a low rumbling from Doug's stomach. He gave me a troubled look and an imperceptible nod as Frieda struggled from the bed. Her long grey hair hung in braids descending over an old plaid shirt and bib overalls. She fumbled into a pair of homemade moccasins and then hobbled to an old trunk at the foot of the bed. It might have been a hope chest sometime in the distant past but was more of a "hopeless" chest now. My heart went out to her.

Doug, in the most courteous voice he could muster, said, "Really, ma'am. We had breakfast just before we got here. You really shouldn't."

Frieda replied, "No, no. It's no bother. I've been needing a cup myself."

She opened the chest and set out three antiquated teacups with mismatched saucers. They looked a bit grimy to me. Doug's stomach grumbled a little louder. Being a good hostess, Frieda proceeded to wipe each cup with a well-used dishcloth which left a few oily streaks in each cup. Doug's stomach rumbled and twitched. Frieda then opened a smoke-stained cabinet and brought out a box of oatmeal cookies. The "best before" date had expired eight or ten years before, and they were hard as rock, but nothing that a good dip in a hot cup of tea wouldn't cure.

I doubt that Doug took more than a tiny sip from his tea, but to his credit, he did eat half a cookie, a truly god-fearing thing to do. The bible says, "Whatsoever is set before you, eat, asking no question for conscience sake." I figure so long as the water's boiled, it won't kill you. Once I got past a couple unidentifiable lumps floating in my cup, I managed to enjoy both the tea and the cookie. I have to admit, part of my enjoyment was watching Doug. Plus, I was learning all kinds of things as Frieda talked on and on. I never realized there were so many types of wild mushrooms. How to avoid the black flies and other bugs that keep tourists out of the woods might come in handy if we ever flee from some war or disaster. I could hardly wait to share her beaver tail recipe with my wife. Frieda said they had more tails than they would ever eat, and I was welcome to take one home.

I admit, I was glad to hear Horst come tromping up the trail. The door flung open, and he stood there eyeing us for a few seconds. People who live in the bush don't have a great deal of trust in strangers and even less for preachers. After we explained our plight, he warmed to us, or it might have been the hundred dollars I pulled from my wallet. We started to get our coats, but Horst slapped a hand on the table.

"First we eat, then we get the moose."

"That's alright," I said. "We just had a cookie and tea. You go right ahead. We'll just wait."

Horst went to a cupboard and dealt four large bowls onto the table. A muddle of spoons and forks stood at attention in a mug at the center. He gently lifted the pot from the stove and placed the stew beside the silverware. To this day I don't know what was in that pot. Scummy blobs of fat floated here and there on the surface. Mysterious shapes of meat and roots lurked in the dark abyss below.

Horst glared at me, "You don't eat with Horst, you don't get your moose!"

Some hospitality is hard to refuse. Horst brought out a large coarse loaf of bread and with his big grimy hands tore off four chunks, placing a piece in each bowl. "Breaking of bread" took on new meaning that day. He handed a large ladle to Doug. Doug wasn't feeling too good, but he was trying to be a good sport. He gently skimmed around the fat and soaked his bread with the hot broth. The ladle then passed to me. That concoction had been on the stove so long there couldn't possibly be a germ or any other living thing in it. I don't know what possessed me, but I took the long-handled dipper and dug right to the bottom of the pot. *If I die, I die.* The old King James says that when Darius saw the handwriting on the wall, he was "astonied." That's the only word that describes the look on Horst's face as I withdrew the ladle. I had scooped up a greasy old rag.

Horst jumped from his seat, grabbed the pot, and quickly placed it into an old washbasin on the counter. "You fool," he said. "you pulled the plug from the hole!"

I turned to look at Doug, but he was already out the door. I could hear the poor man retching into a snowbank. I right nearly joined him, but we needed Horst's help.

There's no point in going into detail about how we managed to get the moose out of the bog. If Caspar didn't like me before, he hated me by the time we left the marsh. With the time and money spent, Doug and I could easily have bought a side of beef. Why shucks, we could have bought the whole animal – cut, wrapped, and delivered.

I DID A great deal of hunting on my own in Saskatchewan, but apart from a few grouse, never put meat in the freezer without a partner. Hunting is sometimes about "going," not always about "getting." Once I climbed a black spruce and sat on a limb overlooking a game trail. The cutest little chickadee landed on the barrel of my rifle. It cocked its head to one side and looked me over, probably thinking, *What are you doing up here?* I suspect it had some insect larvae or spruce seeds hidden away somewhere on the tree. You can learn plenty about wilderness survival from those little birds. Another time, a tiny, short-tailed weasel joined me and ran up the trail staying about ten feet ahead. It was pure white with a little tip of black on its tail. Occasionally it stopped and looked back, likely thinking, *Show me a chicken coup and I'll show you how a pro gets a bird.* One day while I hid in the brush, a magnificent buck nibbled on a willow not ten feet away. I stood up and said, "Boo!" It dropped a pile of scat as it backed up, lowered its antlers, and stared at me with one eye. Thankfully it turned and ran, or I might not be writing this. I sometimes enjoy playing with a "deer stopper." It sounds somewhat like a fawn bleat. One doe that I teased stomped its feet and came closer and closer to investigate. It stopped behind a sapling, with a large ear sticking out on both sides of the tree, thinking I couldn't see it. For me, every day in the wilderness is a good day. When I'm alone in the creation, I feel much closer to the Creator.

JOURNEY TO THE WIND-SWEPT LAND

DRIVING FROM Prince Albert, Saskatchewan to St. John's, Newfoundland is an extraordinary journey. First comes the seemingly endless prairie with field after field of wheat and canola. In eastern Manitoba we entered the forests, lakes, and rock of the Canadian Shield. Our 1976 Ford Pinto huffed and puffed into Thunder Bay, Ontario with a light green Trillium trailer bouncing behind. The Pinto was forest green with large gray blotches of primer from body work I hadn't completed. Reminded me of a large, speckled frog hopping across the country. I repainted it using cans of spray bomb while we took a couple days to visit with old friends. We had quite an audience there in the campground. Anytime someone gave me the "look," I shrugged and thought, *We're from Saskatchewan, what's your excuse.*

That Pinto was the most expensive inexpensive car I've ever owned. It didn't like pulling a trailer and soon blew heavy black smoke. I didn't dare sit and idle for fear of smoke inhalation. By the time we chugged into Sault St. Marie at the eastern end of Lake Superior, I needed a litre of oil at every fill up. Then the starter conked out, which meant a couple days of camping while waiting for repairs. I'm surprised they didn't name the town after the Mosquito Coast. The nights were too hot to keep the windows closed and commando units of mosquitos poured through every little tear or crack in the screens. By two in the morning the night following the starter replacement, I surrendered to the onslaught. We packed the kids into the car and fled to the east. I drove and drove and drove – all the way to Ottawa. I was tired; our boys were hungry; my wife was running out of strategies to keep them calm. I would have stopped sooner, but camp sites failed to materialize along the way. A sign with a large question mark signaled a tourist information center ahead. I followed those question marks, expecting to pull over anytime. I was still following them when we reached downtown Ottawa. That's when a sign, stating "Tourist Information," directed us into an underground parking lot.

THUNK! The kids doubled over in their seatbelts. Lin caught herself on the front dash. I slammed into the steering wheel. The camping trailer had rammed under a steel girder. A large fissure ran from the little kitchen window on one side to the door on the other. We were stuck! The camper tires ballooned to the sides from the extra pressure exerted by the ceiling beam. For a moment I thought I would have to deflate them to back up. There was no going forward. I pulled my

John Deer cap as low over my eyes as possible as a security guard approached. He directed the cars behind me as they backed up the ramp and onto the street. I put the Pinto into reverse and jammed on the gas. The Trillium slowly scraped from under the beam. Backing up a trailer requires much zigzagging on my part, and two blocks of downtown Ottawa traffic were gridlocked by the time we backed onto the street. Horns blared and people stared. *I'm from Saskatchewan...*

Holes in the camper screens were survivable, but not a sprung door and a crack running from the door to the kitchen window. A body shop in Hull, Quebec welcomed us. A couple days were required to complete the repair, which gave us time in a hotel with mosquito free air conditioning, hot showers, and comfortable beds. It was time well spent. We visited the parliament buildings, explored the museums, and strolled along the Rideau Canal. The street vendors, artists, and musicians were delightful.

Our next stop was Montreal. Don't get me wrong, we love Saskatchewan, but the history of explorers like Peter Potts, whose standard translation of long speeches during treaty negotiations was, "He say he damn glad," hardly compared to the exploits of Jacques Cartier and Samuel de Champlain. Trekking the streets of old Montreal is a charming walk into Canadian history.

We arrived in Quebec City during Jean Baptiste Days. Music, dancing, food, and costumes combined to create *joie de vivre* I've not experienced anywhere else. I recall a street clown following a lady opposite us, perfectly miming her every step and gesture. When the woman turned to see why we were laughing, the comic quickly turned and mimicked an unsuspecting victim walking in the opposite direction.

Language was a major issue in Quebec in the 1980s. Some shops refused service in English. Not a problem. I figured that two years of college French and ten years of reading English and French on the back of cereal boxes was all I needed. I learned otherwise when reading my order from a menu to an older waitress. She gawped and said, “qu'est-ce que?” I figured she had probably forgotten her hearing aid and started over. The woman interrupted, “Point s’il vous plait.”

Registering into a campground was even more challenging. There was nothing to point to and I was bound and determined I would not use English. I mangled the language so badly that the camp manager finally pleaded, “Veuillez utilizer l’anglais.” I gave him a vacant stare as though I couldn’t understand. *When in Quebec, do as the Quebecers.* He finally guessed my request and led us to a vacant site. I’m certain I heard sobbing in the dark as he walked away. You have to admire people so passionate about their culture.

MOST OF OUR stretch in the Maritimes was spent in automotive shops. The engine had developed a definite “knock” and was using more oil, a lot more. Stops at gas stations went something like this:

“Fill it with gas and give me two litres of 10-30.”

“Don’t you think I’d better check the oil first?”

“Maybe *after* you add it just to make sure it doesn’t need three.”

Shortly after leaving Baddeck, Nova Scotia where we toured the Alexander Graham Bell Historic Site, the Pinto's starter began to engage only intermittently and sometimes not at all. Out of fear of being stranded, I drove to North Sydney without turning off the engine. Fort Louisburg, Peggy's Cove, and Cape Breton would have to wait for another trip. It was time to get to Newfoundland. No more rebuilds. This time we purchased a new starter.

OUR FIRST MAJOR voyage was on the ferry from North Sydney, Nova Scotia to Port aux Basque, Newfoundland. This was before the high-speed vessels sailing today and, barring rough weather, required a full eight hours to cross. We drove aboard and proceeded to the main deck. Immediately our youngest took off at a run. Three weeks in the back seat of a Ford Pinto is shear torture for a little boy. I yelled, "SEAN!" Four little boys and three men turned to look at me. *What have we done?* When we named our sons, Michael and Sean, it was important that their names be relatively unique in our families. There was only one Michael and no other Seans. I had argued with one of my sisters over the name "Michael." Fortunately, our baby was born first. Our children were born in Saskatchewan in an area predominantly English and Ukrainian. There was the occasional "Mike," but not among any of our friends. I won't even hazard a guess at how many Michaels and Seans live in Newfoundland. The boys fit right in.

I've been seasick several times in my life. Words won't describe what it is like to wretch until you turn inside out. You feel like you are going to die and are powerfully temped to jump overboard and get it over with. We were warned that it would be a rough sailing that night, so I took a double dose of Gravol. There was a definite reek of that indescribable, yet unmistakable odor left by passengers that didn't.

A true Newfoundlander is too practical to book a cabin. He'll book regular seats and roll out the sleeping bags on the floor. We followed that example on future trips but this time, like true "come from aways," booked a small inside cabin. Michael insisted on a top bunk; Sean slept in a lower bunk; Lin and I shared a berth. That was before we reached the open sea and the storm hit. The ferry pitched and turned like a loose car on a roller coaster. Sean rolled into the wall as we went up one side of a wave and rolled off the bed and across the floor as we came down the other – didn't even wake up. I tucked him in with his mother while I checked on Michael. He was clutching the side of the bed frame like a spider gripping a web in a gale. "Dad," he said. "Is it going to sink?"

The night stretched on and on and on. The sea was so rough that we spent three extra hours on open water before making port. The galley was serving breakfast, but there were no takers. I scalded my hand holding my coffee. The black liquid kept slopping over the rim, and I couldn't set it down for fear of it sliding off the table.

When we entered calmer waters our little family marched to the deck to get a glance of our new island home. We had studied pictures of the Long Range Mountains, spectacular fiords, and lush forests of western Newfoundland. Protected beaches and historical sites beckoned. In contrast, we expected eastern Newfoundland to be colder and bleaker, and the trees to be stunted and bent from the incessant North Atlantic wind. As I squinted through the lifting fog, I saw no mountains; no trees; hardly a blade of grass; just barren rocks. *If this is the nicer side of the island, what in the world is the other side like?*

Leaving the terminal, the Pinto “knocked” along a barren stretch of road. Signs picturing semi-trucks being blown over warned of high winds. Thirty minutes later we entered the land we had seen in photos. In future years we would explore the west coast, walk its beaches, and climb its mountains, but it was time to make tracks for St. John’s while there was still life in the old Ford.

TROUTIN'

SEVEN YEARS IN Newfoundland was the adventure of a lifetime. St. John's, with its jellybean-colored houses, old buildings, and colorful history, is a wonder. The French, English, Spanish, and Basque cast their mark onto the land and their nets into the water. Why? Fish! I'd read John Cabot's account from his voyage in 1497. "The sea there is full of fish that can be taken not only with nets but with fishing-baskets." A hundred years later a fishing captain wrote of cod schools "so thick by the shore that we hardly have been able to row a boat through them." That's my kind of fishing! I saw photos of codfish twice the size of my boys and triple the weight.

After moving into our new home and enduring all the frustrating rigamarole required in relocating to a new province, we began our exploration of St. John's with a trip to the wharf. I envisioned a fish market like the one we had visited in Hawaii. I didn't expect to see the colorful fish of the tropics, but the North Atlantic offers cod, lobster, squid, capelin, seal, and other delicacies. What a surprise! No market and no fish. The cod fishery had been on the decline for several years and collapsed before our move back to the mainland. Any fish being caught were sold to fish plants so fishermen could qualify for unemployment benefits during what's called "the long, cold, hungry month of March." I eventually found a fisherman in one of the outports selling fillets from undersized cod, but my fish market dreams were dashed.

I didn't own a boat and knew few people who did. Ocean fishing was out for me, but Newfoundland abounds with small lakes, ponds, and streams. Landlubbers like myself don't need expensive equipment. Basics include a spin caster, a fishing vest, a handful of fishing flies, and a pair of nippers, known as fingernail clippers by the uninitiated. I also had a pair of hip waders for creek fishing. Not being a purist, I occasionally fudged with the addition of a worm.

Roy, a queer hand, that's what they call an easy-go-lucky crew member on a fishing boat, taught me the intricacies of fly fishing à la Newfoundland. Cut about six inches off a broomstick and insert a small eyebolt in each end. Attach one end to the line coming from your pole and tie a leader to the other. The leader can be any length, but five or six feet, depending on the length of your pole, makes it easy to reel in. Tie a fly to the end and you're set. I sometimes tied as many as four flies at varying distances on the leader and once hooked three trout on one cast. To be honest, a dozen that size wouldn't have filled the frying pan but it's about the fishing, not the eating. Your spin caster will wing that rig halfway across a small pond. As you reel in, the homemade bobber jiggles and bounces through the water giving the flies good wiggle action. As I recall, the daily limit on trout thirty years ago was around twenty.

I traveled throughout the province and carried fishing gear in the trunk of the car for those occasions that I had extra time. Several creeks come to mind. One was a small stream I passed while driving up the Great Northern Peninsula. Brook trout aren't very big, but a fish is waiting in every little swirl and pool. I slipped on my gumboots, attached a black gnat to my line and hiked about ten yards through thick brush to a small opening. I had bites on the first cast, four or five on each finger and three on both thumbs. I've never seen mosquitos like Newfoundland mosquitoes. Well... There was this one time in northern Minnesota when I feared getting out of the car. The ornery things were crawling up the air vents by the time I backed out of the brush. Can you believe it? I had thirty bites on one ankle! It's hard to hook a fish while crashing through the willows trying to escape the bugs.

I came across a gorgeous stream on a trip northwest of Gander. A small waterfall fell into a large, deep pool. A good trail bordered the bank. I parked the car, donned my boots, and assembled my rod. Five minutes later I had a nice brooky. As I retrieved the hook, I got the oddest feeling. This was a perfect place to fish – close to the road, easy access, nice rocks for sitting – but no angling artifacts. No cigarette butts littered the ground. No broken line hung from the shrubs. No squashed beer cans lined the trail. No blackened rocks testified to mug-ups of tea. I noticed a glint of metal through the trees and crept up for a look. A FISH HATCHERY! Time to skedaddle.

That could have been an expensive trout. Speaking of, I still had the fish. My sense of morality wouldn't allow me to toss it. "You catch it, you eat it." Only problem, I wouldn't be home for two days. Keeping a fish in the trunk of the car wouldn't be tenable. That evening I pulled into an outport for a room and walked to a small café. A fellow came to take my order and I said, "Any chance of you cooking a trout for me?" I love those fellows from around the bay. Newfoundlanders are my kind of people! They perfectly understand where I'm coming from. Wasting a good trout would be unconscionable. The fish was tiny by Newfoundland standards, but nothing could have tasted better.

Just once have I eaten what I refer to as the thousand-dollar fish platter. We were camping on the edge of a sheltered bay where a small stream pours over a large boulder into a pool that empties into the Atlantic. Lin was fixing supper; the boys were exploring the campground; I was flicking my line into that pool. WHAM! I thought I had a whopper. It turned out to be ten inches of muscled flipper and fin. The fish was a beautiful silver color, not at all similar to a speckled trout. I caught five more before going back to camp. They made a delightful meal. Later I found out I was catching salmon fry. If a game warden had happened along, the fine would have been stiff, and ignorance is not a good defense. *Lessons to self: always check the regulations, know your species, and know where you're fishing.*

"YOU'RE ALWAYS talking about building a canoe," chided my newest hunting buddy, Dave. "Here's some plans. I'll help you build the strongback to get started." Those words began a two-year project in my basement. I wouldn't build just any canoe. I chose to build a sixteen-foot laker with a flat bottom, belled sides, and a thirty-eight-inch beam. That design is almost impossible to capsize and requires two people at the paddles. When finished it was suitable for a family of four with all its camping gear or two men and a moose. The sides were formed from pine strips, accented with cedar. The gunnels were cut from mahogany and the seats from oak. I sawed, glued, and sanded every piece. The seats were hand woven. A thin cover of fiberglass inside and out finished the project.

The craft looked like a piece of furniture. It should have. I could have refurnished our entire living room with what I spent. Each strip for the sides was one inch wide, one quarter inch thick, and the length of a twelve-foot board. I burnt out my table saw while cutting them. You can imagine how many strips are needed to construct a canoe. The glitch was the keel. Normally the keel is attached after the fiberglass is finished. That way it can be removed and replaced as it wears. I attached it before the fiberglass, creating extra work. *Lesson to self: It isn't cheating to read the instructions before starting a project. You'll end up reading them sooner or later.*

The biggest problem was getting it out of the basement. *Duh?!* The sides of the canoe belled out to forty inches. The basement door was only thirty-five inches wide. Making an even greater challenge, the room was forty feet long, but only fifteen feet wide. The door opened into a cement pit three feet below ground level. The depth of the canoe was only two feet, or it would never have come out. For a fearful moment I thought it would be staying in the basement as a permanent ornament.

THERE'S NO BETTER time for a little father-son bonding than when your wife is spending a couple weeks with her mother. And no better way than a canoe trip into the wilderness. Surely the *big* fish are waiting where no car has driven and no man has trod. The canoe was too heavy for one person to carry but I figured that two sons, ages ten and six, are equal to one man. W*rong!*

I picked a small lake along the highway going to Marystown. It looked like the perfect place to launch an adventure. The connecting lakes I saw on a map must surely lead to an ice cooler full of fresh trout. We parked; off came the canoe; out came the camping gear. Cloudy skies and a brisk wind warned of coming rain. No problem. That's why rubber boots and rain slickers were invented. The first lake was our maiden voyage. Two little boys don't quite equal their dad on the paddles, so we zigzagged our way to the first portage. Neither do two little boys equal a man carrying one end of the canoe. I hardly did myself, but we managed to lift, push, and drag my formerly beautiful craft down a trail and halfway across a bog toward the second lake. Then the wind stopped, and a light drizzle began. Next came the mosquitoes and the black flies. Three large servings of their favorite meal were grunting and panting an invitation to supper. There was no escape. Within minutes Sean screamed and blindly ran down the trail flailing his arms through a cloud of black flies. *What kind of father would do this to his children?* Mike forlornly blinked through the trickles of water running down his face. We were halfway across the bog, almost to where I wanted to camp. To continue meant half a bog to get there and a full bog to return. I ran after Sean and put a blanket over his head.

We retreated: dragging, pulling, and pushing the canoe in the direction we had come from. After we entered the trees, I stopped at the first semi-flat clearing. Between the onslaught of mosquitoes and the increasing drizzle, it was time to pitch the tent. What a relief once the screens were zipped and the bugs were zapped. This was home for the next two days. Rain is a fact of life on the Rock, so I had packed some tent projects. We spent time reading and playing games. By the time the clouds cleared, Sean and I had each completed a set of homemade moccasins. Michael had finished a wallet that he kept as a memento for the next thirty years. When the clouds cleared, the tent came down and the gear was packed into the canoe. There was more grunting and straining – and a few minced oaths – as we retreated to the first lake.

With three days remaining to our trip, we pitched camp on a sandy peninsula that jutted out like a small island. Crosswinds eliminated the mosquitoes and blackflies. A deep pool along one side was ideal for swimming. The boys built a fort and had a grand time swimming and digging. We named the spot after the television show, *Gilligan's Island.*

It may have been my cooking, or it may have been the flu. Both sons woke about two a.m. on our final morning with stomach cramps. Soon retching and heaving erupted on both sides of me. The smell nearly caused a sympathy upchuck on my part. Fun time was over. I took down camp and managed to zigzag across the lake to the car. Home was several hours away.

I believe the only way to "hook" little boys on fishing is to "hook" little fish. We had passed a trout farm on our way out of St. John's. The very thought of paying by the inch for what should be free for the taking rubs me wrong, but I calculated that I had enough cash to pay for each boy to catch two fish. That's not a great deal of fishing joy but might be sufficient to salvage the trip. As we approached the troutin' sign I pulled off the road and woke both boys from their sleeping bags in the back seat.

"Wake up," I said. "We're going to catch some fish."

Sean opened and quickly closed one eye. Michael squinted, rolled his eyes, and pulled a blanket over his head. I glumly pulled back on the highway. It was time to go home. Later that summer they insisted that we take their mom to "Gilligan's Island." Thoughtful little guys, they were. Sean built a latrine for Lin where she could have the comfort of privacy. I can still envision a roll of toilet paper hanging on a broken tree limb.

The love of my life helping with...

A two-year work of love

Sean and I, ready to launch

I'VE NEVER SEEN a Newfoundlander fishing off the dock with a rod and reel. It's just not done. Nobody had told me that and, being a come from away, it seemed the natural thing to do. I drove my boys and Mark, the next-door neighbor kid, to Portugal Cove. We hiked to the wharf and soon had our first cunner, a blue Atlantic perch that abounds in the waters around the docks. Fishing was so good that I set my rod down and just watched the boys reel in perch after perch. We were a happy lot. Even caught one little flounder.

A young lad sat atop a dock piling scrutinizing our activity. After about ten minutes he ambled over to look at our catch.

"You want to give it a go?" I said.

He gave me a look of astonishment. "Ya're not goin' to eat those are ya?"

"And why wouldn't we?"

"Do ya know what they eats?"

"Can't say as I do," I replied.

"They eats *poop*! Ya'd have to be daft to eat those." With that, he strode off shaking his head.

I had expected that with the cleaning tables located on the dock and the offal thrown into the water, there would be schools of fish lurking around the pilings. It reminded me of fishing behind the slaughterhouse in Payette as a boy. A dim light flickered through the fishing fog of my brain. *All the waste* in a coastal fishing hamlet flows into the sea. The boy's words kept playing through my mind. Suddenly I realized that "poop" was not a metaphor. A large pipe canted down a rock face and into the sea right next to the wharf.

Mark, Mike, and Sean – a happy lot of "Newfie" fishermen

As I continued with the work at hand, I noticed a van load of Asians observing us. Soon they clambered onto the dock. They spoke little English, and the only Asian I know comes from Chinese restaurants and Japanese cars. Their driver held up a camera and in broken English explained that they wanted to photograph some *authentic* Newfoundland fishermen. Somewhere in Japan there's a photo of two boys that were born in Saskatchewan and one that was born in England holding a string of cunners. Underneath is the probable caption, *Newfoundland Fishermen.*

The perch fillets were firm and white with a mild, slightly sweet flavor. I hadn't tasted anything like them. The sweetness kind of bothered me. *Do ya know what they eats?* That was our one and only time fishing off the dock.

THE FOG WAS burning off a calm sea. No need for Gravol as we boarded the ferry to Bell Island. My dad had driven from Oregon: 4,583 miles requiring 77 hours and 42 minutes of driving. Our first experience of cod jigging awaited. Bill Whalen, a Bell Island resident, had invited us for a morning on the sea. We missed the early ferry and arrived around 10:00. The old outboard moaned a "pop, whoosh, whoosh, whoosh, pop..." as we sputtered to the cod jigging ground. Other fishermen were already coming in, their fish boxes empty. The cod hadn't been "eatin' the rocks" that morning. "Fishing" and "catching" are two different things. You can have a great day on the water and not have a nibble. We continued to the fishing ground, enjoying Bill's yarns, and learning about cod.

The normally grey Atlantic was translucent green. Lazy, gentle swells gently lifted and lowered the boat in the water. A humpback whale arched its back in greeting about thirty yards from where we drifted with the current – a sure sign of marine life in the waters. A massive jellyfish undulated past, its tentacles streaming behind. The body resembled a large pulsating brain. We couldn't have planned a better outing for my dad.

We were in the North Atlantic, a thousand miles from the coast of Maine, and what do we see in the water? Cans, plastic jugs, and old bottles – the flotsam and jetsam of consumerism washed to sea from the mainland.

Back to cod jigging. A cod jigger is a pound of lead molded in the shape of a six-inch fish resembling a herring. Two large, needle-sharp hooks project from the mouth. A heavy line is attached through a hole in the tail. We dropped our jigs over the side, let them sink to the bottom, and began a jigging motion with our wrists. *Wham!* "Fish on!" What a day. Last boat on the water; last boat to return; only boat with a good catch. God was smiling on us. We brought home sixty pounds of fish from which we took thirty-five pounds of fillets.

Waiting at the dock were a half dozen older men and women.

"What have ya got fer us, Billy?"

"Just ya wait," Bill replied. "Ya can have the heads, britches, and livers. But I want the tongues for me friend."

Bill explained the terrible state of some communities. People struggled to accumulate enough "stamps" to get unemployment checks; went on welfare when the checks ran out; waited for a short-turn government work project; and then repeated the process. He called it "survival." The province sponsored regional trade schools in various communities. That kept people busy but didn't provide jobs. As one fellow told me, "I've taken three apprenticeship programs. Now I need five years of experience so someone will hire me." The poverty was oppressive.

That afternoon the provincial economy was the furthest thing from our minds as we feasted on fried cod tongues and hash browns. A cod tongue is the fleshy nugget of fish from the underside of a cod's jaw that reminds me of a fried oyster. Mmm, mmm! My dad never forgot that trip or those people. Bill gave him a hand-crafted model fishing boat as a souvenir. Today it hangs from the ceiling in my shop.

I managed cod jigging excursions with two other friends before we left Newfoundland. Roger, the manager of a small general store in a community on the north coast of the island, was an efficiency expert extraordinaire. He had his favorite fishing spot where he had calculated the average depth. He had then cut a piece of line that reached the bottom, stretched across his dory, and hung a couple feet down the opposite side. By attaching a jig to both ends of the line, he could pull a cod up on the port side of the dory while lowering a jig over the starboard. Roger didn't waste any action. When we returned to the dock, a large pail, salt, and cutting table awaited. The catch was curing within minutes. I prefer a more relaxed form of fishing, but I was impressed. Now I understand where the Newfoundland saying, "a single line may have two hooks," came from.

Dave and Blanche Smith took my wife and me fishing on the south side of the Avalon Peninsula near the bird sanctuary at Cape St. Mary's. Thousands of gulls, razorbills, common murres, kittiwakes, gannets, and cormorants nest on the rocks and cliffs in the area. More than 20,000 birds make it their home in the winter. We decided to have a cookout on a tiny island of rock and gravel. Now that's the proper way to enjoy a fresh catch. Someone had been there earlier robbing nests and smashing the eggs on the rocks. I was appalled! I enjoy hunting and fishing, but Mother Earth and her bounty deserve respect and care.

SKIPPER TOM

NEWFOUNDLAND HAS MORE moose on the loose than anyplace I know. And the province has the fairest draw system I've seen for managing its moose population. We lived in St. John's, the largest city in the Province. To hunt in areas on the Avalon Peninsula, you will wait several years as you proceed from the lower pools of applications to the top of the list. The system guarantees that everyone eventually gets an opportunity. If you don't mind sharing with a buddy and are willing to drive inland to a remote part of the island, you can get a license every year. My buddy Dave and I always studied the numbers and made the trek to the island interior. Dave did most of the shooting. I did the driving and supplied the camper.

The province has the strictest gun control I've experienced, and I've lived in Idaho, Oregon, Texas, British Columbia, Saskatchewan, and Ontario. Sport shooting took place through clubs or by special permit.

Every time I sighted in my rifle, I was required to apply for a permit stating date, time, and place. If caught carrying a firearm outside of the hunting season without a permit, you were deemed to be hunting and the penalty was stiff. It was my understanding that .22 rifles had been banned for general use. I guess too many insulators were being shot off the telephone poles.

That didn't deter boys from grouse and rabbit hunting. It was common in the outports to see young fellows traipsing into the woods carrying a small hatchet and a roll of wire. They were adept at setting snares. Many a time I came across little guys along the backroads who had constructed crude tripods of branches from which hung braces of rabbits or grouse – a good way to make a few dollars from passing motorists. Depending on the season, you could sometimes buy cod tongues or berries from similar young entrepreneurs.

In the 1980s, fish and game officers didn't carry firearms in Newfoundland. Officers knew the men in their areas and had sometimes grown up in the local community. One explained to me that his purpose was not to eliminate poaching, but to keep it at a minimum. He'd let fishermen know approximately when he'd be checking the docks to inspect their equipment and look over their catch. He never snuck up on fellows in the woods, but he expected hunters to have a license and to obey the rules. He'd turn somewhat of a blind eye on bay boys trying to feed their families. Fish and wild game were staples for many rural families. I recall a restaurant in Burgeo that served moose and rabbit. I have my doubts that it was government inspected and I knew not to ask. *"Whatsoever is set before you, eat, asking no question for conscience sake..."* was good enough for old King James, and it's good enough for me.

THE OLD TIMERS are survivors and know all the tricks of getting around the rules. With unemployment running up to ninety percent in some outports, fudging on the regulations wasn't considered a moral issue. *The Lord helps them which helps themselves...just don't get caught.*

Skipper Tom, an old greybeard from Nergens Cove, took it on himself to teach me some tricks of the trade. I had been invited for a cup of tea after officiating a funeral. Soon talk got around to fishing and hunting, and Skipper invited me to his basement for a tot of Screech. We canted down a steep, narrow staircase. A single bulb dangling from two wires in the ceiling cast eerie shadows of nets and jigs, old harpoons, and buoys. Hand carved needles and shuttles hung on the wall. Skipper had spent many a winter repairing nets and gear. Right in the middle of the room was a huge boulder. It protruded about four feet out of the floor and was probably eight feet across.

Skipper Tom explained, "When we built the house, that one was too big to move, so we built around it. Me father was still alive at the time. We logged the lumber ourselves; cut the trees in the winter; milled the boards in the spring. Buddy down the road has a small sawmill. Tried to get the frame up in the fall so's we could work on the inside through the winter. Took a couple years but when we finished, she was paid for. Man can't get by except he owns his own home."

I took a closer look at the open rafters and studs. I've never seen two-by-fours so warped and twisted. The house had gone up while the wood was still green. The stairs were narrow and tilted slightly to the left going down. I found out later that many houses in the outports were without title. People just built wherever there was a piece of land close to the water. Often they built a second house behind the first for their children, a kind of "weaning" house. Building codes were enforced in communities like St. John's but were lacking or largely ignored in the remote coves and bays. Tom motioned toward a stool by his work bench. "Sit. I'll pour ye a tot. This ain't that watered-down Screech comes from St. John's. I gets this from a b'y 'round the cove. Twill stiffen the tar on ya're shingles."

One sip and I gasped for breath. My lips burned and my eyes watered. Whooee! It could have been used as paint stripper. Whooee!

Two shotguns hung on the wall above the work bench. The upper gun was an old Scottish double barrel twelve bore with pin fire. One of the Damascus barrels was split. The old guns weren't designed for today's smokeless powders. The other gun was a well-worn Model 37 single shot 12-gauge.

"Let me tell ya 'bout huntin' round the bay here." Skipper took a swig of rum. "First t'ing is figurin' out what the game warden's up to. He generally sticks to a pattern. Any chucklehead gets pinched deserves it for bein' foolish. Second t'ing, always fill your store the week before huntin' season opens. 'Tis far easier to get those ducks and terrs before they get spooked. Let me show ya a trick I use when I don't get me moose draw."

On old Tom's work bench were a couple boxes of shotgun shells, a tin coffee can half full of shotgun bbs, and a second can with a handful of lead balls. Judging from an old mold and other tools, it looked like Tom was making bullets for a muzzleloader.

"Watch," he said. He picked up a 12-gauge shotgun shell and carefully pried open the crimped end with his pocketknife. He poured the bbs into the coffee can. He then picked up a lead ball and inserted it into the shell, folded the crimp into the mouth of the shell, and sealed it with candle wax.

"What do ya t'ink? Looks like a regular 12-gauge shell filled with number six shot for grouse or rabbits, don't it? And that's what the game warden t'inks if he comes across me in the woods. Of course, I'll have a pocket full of regular shells. I'm not above shootin' a rabbit. But these are me special moose loads.

"I know what you're t'inkin', but there ain't no command *in the Bible* 'bout shootin' a moose outa season. 'Tis only a sin if ya gets caught."

Tom poured another round of rum. He took a small swig and looked at me, the lone bulb reflecting from his eyes as he mournfully shook his head.

"Problem with government these days, they're always changin' the rules. Makes it impossible to keep the law. Have to be a lawyer to understand the regulations. 'Bout twenty year ago this here government fella in St. John's comes up with the idea that moose should only be hunted at night with a spotlight. Can ya imagine that? He figures a moose won't run with a light shinin' in his eyes. That way a hunter can walk right up to him, drop him in his tracks, and not wound the poor t'ing. Only t'ing was, you was only allowed one shot. That way you'd be certain to make it count, and the moose wouldn't suffer none. Here in Nergens Cove we found that real funny. Apart from the one-shot rule, we'd been huntin' that way for years."

It seemed logical to me at the time, but just about anything seems logical after a tot of moonshine.

"Never forget that year," Tom continued. "I tied me torch, what you'd call a flashlight, to the side of me rifle, walked up the road, and turned down a trail leadin' to the bog. Always a moose or two hangin' out there. Wasn't twenty minutes when I hear trompin' in the brush. Ain't no question when a moose is roamin' around. I wait. It comes closer and closer. I switch on me torch. There he is, this big old moose, with a dumb look on his face, flappin' his eyelids at the light. I t'ink to me self, 'Just one shot. Got to make it count.' I take me time and lean against a tree to steady me aim. Just at that moment a rabbit bolts from the brush. I musta jumped three feet. The gun went off and the moose took off.

"It was enough to make a preacher cuss. Well, maybe not in your case. Made me hoppin' mad I tells ya. I start walkin' up the path and hadn't gone thirty yards when low and behold, there's Mr. Moose, standin' in the middle of the trail. I thought to meself, 'at night, with a light, and only one shot.' 'Tis dark as a witch's cat; no stars in sight; couldn't see the moon; and not a light anywhere. What's the chance of a game warden wanderin' in the dark near Nergens Cove? Once again, I take me time and lean against a tree to steady me aim. Bang! Right between the eyes.

"Flash! A light as bright as a locomotive lamp is in me face. The trees show plain as day for a mile around. I'm nearly blind and feelin' like that moose felt just before I pulled the trigger. 'Tis the game officer, real as life, peekin' from behind a spruce."

"Got ya this time," he says. "Ya know the law. One shot, and I heard two."

"No. No sir," I replies. "I only shot once. Musta been an echo, or maybe somebody's truck backfirin'."

"We'll see, won't we," he says. "Let me have a gander."

"I was beginnin' to think he was goin' to do an autopsy on that moose. I mean, the hole between his eyes was as plain as the nose on your face. But that didn't suit the warden. He ran his light down the moose's back. Checked its rib cage. Ran his hands down each leg."

"What's this?" he asks. "There's a fresh hole through this front hoof. I know a second shot when I hear it, and this proves it. Got ya!"

"No b'y I says. Just one shot."

He shines the light in me face. "How do you explain that this moose has two bullet holes?"

"Funny t'ing," I says. "I was shinin' me light in his face and just as I pulled the trigger, he raised his hoof to shield his eyes. Tryin' to see who I was, I reckon. Bullet went right through his foot and smacked him in the head."

I started choking on a swallow of rum and thought I might choke to death right there in Skipper's basement. He took a swig from his jar and winked at me, "You don't think I'd lie to a preacher?"

THE CRAZIEST HUNTING I've experienced was for inshore seal. This was limited to fishermen who lived along the coast and were hunting mature seals for meat. Skipper Tom thought it would be a good experience for a come from away like myself and invited me to join him and his grandson, Winston. It's a spring hunt which takes place by boat when the ice is breaking up around the northern inlets and bays. Some ice pans are large enough for a man to walk on. In fact, in some of the small bays and inlets, the kids play a game called "copying". It's similar to "follow the leader" with the lead child jumping from one block of ice to the next. A good way to fall in the water and drown, if you ask me.

Skipper Tom owned an open dory with an old Merc outboard. Winston was at the tiller, I sat at the bow, and Skipper stood with his legs braced on either side of the center seat so he could survey the open water. He handed me an old British Enfield. Forty or fifty years of sea air hadn't been kind to it. We idled around what reminded me of giant irregular ice cubes in an ocean-sized pitcher.

"Now keep your eyes open," said Tom. "He'll pop his head to see where we're to. Ya shoot and Winston will motor us over so I can gaff him. Got to get there before he sinks."

Up to that point I hadn't thought about what it would be like to shoot a seal. It wasn't long before a seal popped its bald head out of the water. Looked like a little man staring at me.

"Shoot," whispered Tom. "Don't let him get away. I'm ready with the gaff."

I took aim. The seal blinked its shiny black eyes at me. It reminded me of a stuffy we had for one of my boys. Cute little thing. I just couldn't bring myself to shoot it.

"What ya waitin' for? Shoot!"

I aimed high. Better to give the appearance of a poor shot than carry the guilt of shooting that seal. POW! The seal dived. Skipper Tom let out an expletive.

"Give me the gun and you take the gaff," he said. "You townies can't do anyt'ing right. Let me show ya how to shoot."

We continued slowly motoring around the ice pans. *Vroom. VROOM.* Sounds of a boat were approaching from behind. Suddenly a half dozen old doters[5] went porpoising past, skimming the surface of the water like stones skipping across a pond. Right behind them a twenty-foot boat careened around an ice pan in pursuit. Standing atop the cabin, one arm locked around the mast and the other cradling a rifle, a hunter was yelling directions to the helmsman. *Only in Newfoundland.* In all my years of hunting, I've never seen fellows have so much fun.

---

[5] A *doter* is an old seal.

There were no seals for us that day. Skipper Tom tells me I have to come again, that I haven't lived until I've had a good plate of seal flipper. He says flippers look like little hands when they're fried up; that getting the meat off a bone is just like sucking your finger. Some "delicacies" I can live without.

DUSTY AND THE BEAR

MOOSE AND GRIZZLIES of the Chilcotins haunt my hunting fantasies. It's my friend Liam's fault. I was a church pastor in Prince Albert, Saskatchewan and Liam ministered a church in North Battleford. Working with people day in and day out can get to you. I sometimes joked that to keep my sanity I needed to kill something once in a while. Like many of my ministerial friends, I was right into hunting and fishing.

You can imagine how I felt when Liam phoned and asked, "Hey Terry, what would you think of a moose hunt in British Columbia?"

"Why would I do that, Liam? I can drive thirty miles north of Prince Albert and do all the moose hunting I want."

"Yea, but it wouldn't be like spending ten days on horseback with a guide.

"And just how would I do that on a pastor's salary?"

"Good news. Nick Lambert, a friend of the family, owns a ranch in the Chilcotins. He runs a guide and outfitting business in the winter, is a member of our denomination, and every year takes a few church and college officials hunting. He considers it a sort of free will offering for all the blessings of the preceding year. An evangelist from the states just dropped out of this year's hunt and there's a horse and bunk available. All you have to do is contribute to the gas, bring your own food, and pick up a gift for the guide."

To put things in perspective, Nick had clients from the U.S. that would pay thousands for a similar trip. My financial state is such that I don't even read guide and outfitting ads. I'm strictly a meat hunter and can hardly afford a box of bullets. I didn't even own a good hunting knife when Liam called.

I consulted with my wife, and bless her heart, she agreed that it was time to dust off the MasterCard and splurge a little. That meant driving to a big sporting goods store in Saskatoon. For me it was like a trip to Disneyland. To my credit, I tried to exercise control in the actual buying. Here's the list: heavy wool long johns; a Buck clasp knife, considered safer and more comfortable than a Bowie knife when hunting horseback; two rifle scabbards, one for myself and one as gift for the guide; a wool blanket to insert into my sleeping bag; a bullet pouch for my belt; and a box of premium ammunition. Considering all the other expenses in hunting, ammunition is not something to cheap out on. Since wool will keep you warm even when wet and is also quiet when walking through brush, I made a trip to a thrift store to buy an old wool suit. There's no way I'd spend a hundred bucks on a pair of wool pants for a hunting trip.

As to groceries, I tried to stick to the four basic food groups: the beer group, the chip group, the fatty group, and the excessively sweet group. I mean, this was the trip of a lifetime.

NEITHER LIAM NOR I could afford to stay in motels, so we drove and drove and drove until we came to Williams Lake, British Columbia. There we picked up James MacDougal, a college chancellor, who had flown in from the states. Out of "uniform" he was known as Mac. Liam's older sister, Marlene Winters, who lived in Williams Lake, put us up for a couple days while we bought hunting licenses and caught up on sleep.

Marlene and her husband, Ted, were a wonderful couple. At first sight Ted like to scared me to death. He resembled a character from a Stephen King novel. A bloody red scar ran across his forehead and ugly white stitch marks tracked from his left ear to his chin. About a third of the hair was missing on his head. Just the year before a hunter had placed the carcass of a dead calf in a thicket as bait for a grizzly bear, not a very sporting thing to do if you ask me. Worse, he failed to post a warning on the trail. As luck would have it, Ted was deer hunting that fall and followed a trail right to the bait. A grizzly was hiding in the brush, keeping an eye on the dead calf. A growl, a lunge, a swipe of the paw and Ted was down. He immediately curled into a fetal position, tight as a pill bug, with his hands locked behind his neck. The bruin locked onto his head. Smelly old teeth pealed the skin and hair off his scalp.

The grizzly batted and rolled Ted around the thicket like a cat playing with a mouse. Ted managed to stay conscious, played dead, and prayed to high heaven. The bear, thinking Ted was dead, stopped mauling him and dug a shallow depression. It nosed him into the hole and covered him with leaves and dirt. Nothing tastes better to a bruin than meat that's been ripened for a day or two.

Ted waited for what seemed half an eternity before crawling out. He hadn't waited long enough. The bruin was keeping watch and pounced on the poor guy, furious that he might get away. Again, Ted found himself bitten and mauled. For a second time he was covered with leaves and moss and broken limbs. With the loss of blood and the onset of shock, he realized his time was limited. This was a waiting game, and he couldn't wait much longer. As the dark crept in and the stars peeped through the clouds, the bear left. Ted pulled himself out of the brush and drug himself up the trail. Thank God for the CB radio in his truck. He would never have managed the drive home. Grizzlies hadn't even crossed my mind until he told his story. They wouldn't be far out of mind for the next two weeks.

AS WE DROVE through the remote wilds of the Chilcotins, thoughts of bears were soon replaced with fantasies of shooting a moose worthy of the Boon and Crocket Club. Liam's van finally lumbered up to the Lambert's ranch. I had never seen anything like it. The barn was constructed from lumber that had been hand sawn. Nick told us that his father had spent entire winters pulling one end of a rip saw with his uncle pulling the other end as they cut one board after another. With a team of horses they had managed to haul large logs across a frame allowing one man to pull the saw from above and the other from below. They cut beams and boards of various sizes and lengths depending on the width and length of each log. By the end of one winter Nick's father could do a hundred pull-ups with one arm. They don't make men like that today.

Fourteen skulls lined the support beam of the large double doors of the barn. Their vacant stares bore witness to grizzlies that Nick had killed over the years. I had a problem with that. Seemed a shame to kill such magnificent animals. My view would soon mellow.

Eight horses milled about the coral. Five contentedly munched away at a hay bunk on the north end. Three others moved their heads in tandem watching me walk past. One, a broad backed buckskin named Dusty, seemed to give me the "evil" eye.

The Lambert's ranch had a power line and a phone line, one of those party lines that allows every rancher within fifty miles to listen to your "private" conversations, and little else of the modern conveniences. The house was originally constructed from logs and later expanded with rough-hewn lumber. It was sturdy and had housed two generations. One large room encompassed the kitchen, dining area, and living room. A huge woodstove served for cooking and also heated a large hot water tank. Adjacent to the stove sat a long rectangular dining table. It took little imagination to picture a ranch crew tromping in during the fall round-up. Most of the chairs in the common area were draped with black, white, or mottled sheep skins. At first I thought they were for decoration. Once the sun went down and the fire burned low, the practical warmth of the wool would be greatly appreciated. I looked in awe at the head mount of a spectacular bull moose that graced one wall. The resplendent pelt of a majestic silver-tip grizzly lay before the hearth. The room reflected every hunter's dream lodge.

The guest rooms were originally one large open space with bunks for cowboys. At some point dividers had been constructed to form a series of cubicles, each furnished with a bed, side table, and a few pegs on one wall. The old metal-framed beds with stretched wire springs and four-inch mattresses must have felt like heaven to men coming in from a cold day punching cattle.

There was no indoor plumbing. That would have been somewhat pointless considering the depth of the frost in winter. So unless you planned multiple trips, you "held it" as long as possible before heading out the back door, across a small creek, and up a trail to the privy. I have never understood why old outhouses have two seats. Is one for sitting and the other for standing, a kind of "his" and "her" thing? The Old Farmer's Almanac that hung on the wall intrigued me. I started to read an article only to find that several pages had been torn out. A few minutes later when I couldn't find any toilet paper, it dawned on me that the magazine was meant for more than entertainment.

Liam shared an interesting story about the outhouse. He and his wife, Christina, had visited the

Lambert's the previous summer. Sooner or later everyone pays a call to the privy, though men occasionally cheat and go behind a tree. Christina had made her way out the kitchen door, across the creek, and up the trail. She paused, realizing that the facility was in use. The door suddenly swung open and there sat Lucille. "Come on in," she yammered. "It's a two-seater!" Mountain folks sure know how to make you feel at home.

Lucille was the first real ranch woman I ever met. She had no pretensions, and in addition to cooking for a full outfit of cowboys, could also ride a horse, shoot a gun, and gut a deer. On our second day at the ranch we were enlisted to move cattle from an upper pasture to the home place. When we went to saddle the horses, there was Lucille. She was sitting on a little mustang with her six-month-old baby strapped to her chest. Lucille was trail boss for the day.

I was given, you guessed right, Dusty. He was about as lazy as a mule. I swear he had my number. If you've ever experienced one of those "trail-ride" horses that won't go faster than a turtle crossing the road, then you've ridden one of Dusty's cousins. I've had more exciting rides on coin operated ponies at the supermarket. I'm an experienced rider and have done a little wrangling but no matter how I shouted, kicked, and swatted, Dusty was determined to be last in line. He was always covered in dust from the other horses. He was just plain "dusty." The more I yelled at him, the more Lucille yelled at me. She wasn't just the trail boss; she was downright bossy.

Come supper time, we sat down to a meal fit for a lumberjack. One inch sirloin steaks, mashed potatoes drenched with thick, heavy gravy, and home-grown carrots filled our plates. Fresh made bread, cut in one-inch slices, was slathered with ranch churned butter. I had a hard time cleaning my plate. but so as not to offend Lucille, I forced myself to eat a second helping of everything. Then she pulled a huckleberry pie from the oven, cut a hefty man slice for each of us, and encouraged us to smother it with fresh cream. I thought I had died and gone to heaven, and later that night I nearly did from heartburn and indigestion.

After supper we moved to the living room. Flames leapt in a primitive dance in the large fireplace. The eyes of the moose glinted mournfully through the flickering shadows. The bear rug radiated warmth and warning. Its massive teeth and enormous claws held untold stories of predator and prey. One look convinced me that only a miracle had saved Ted Winters from a painful death. Nick poured everyone a cup of hot buttered rum. Evenings were for stories and yarns of the wild. Naturally, the conversation centered on hunting. The fourteen skulls over the barn door intrigued me. I started to say my piece about conservation but was cut off by Lucille.

"You city boys say what you will, but you've never seen a ewe with her udder ripped off and her lamb left to starve. You've never had to drive off the coyotes from the mess left by a grizzly. Some years we lose as many as four horses. Every calf lost to those critters is money out of pocket. There ain't no place for bears on a ranch. We're not runnin' a game preserve, ya know. If they want to live, best to stay on their own side of the mountain. Same goes for wolves and eagles."

I've never met people who hated predators so much. But then I've never lost a flock of sheep, a good horse, or a crop of calves. I believe "there's a place for everything, and everything needs to stay in its place." The problem comes when something is not in its place. Makes you think. Still, I had to ask about those skulls I'd seen at the barn.

Nick assured me that they were all "problem" bears. Five had been shot with a handgun at short range. That got us off topic. Call it a guy thing, but men are obsessed with guns. Nick explained that American hunters had given him several pistols over the years as gifts for good hunts. Truth be told, once they found out the laws in Canada, they were probably a bit shy of getting caught with handguns on their way home. Nick's favorite was a Smith and Wesson 44 Magnum with an eight and three eighths inch barrel. The 44 had both speed and impact. Getting hit with one would be like having a fist drive through your chest at eight hundred miles an hour. A direct hit will stop just about anything.

Nick turned the conversation back to bears. "Grizzlies are pretty predictable. In some ways I'd rather go after a grizzly than a black bear. You never know what a black bear will do, but nine times out of ten I can tell you what to expect from a grizzly. Once he knows he's bein' followed, he'll circle around and come up from behind. Then it's a question of who's doin' the huntin' and who's bein' hunted. You have to watch yourself. That old bruin will come up quietly. You'll never outrun him, and you won't have time to climb a tree. Given a choice I'll take a pistol over a rifle if I'm in heavy brush. If Mr. Bear comes at ya, start shootin'. If he don't drop, jump to the side and keep shootin' as he runs by. Don't stop shootin' till he stops movin', you run out of bullets, or...well, we won't talk about that."

Suddenly my attitude about bears in the wild changed. I imagined myself with an oversized handgun blasting away at a twelve-hundred-pound rabid grizzly, jumping to the side, and bringing it down inches from my feet. The more likely scenario would be dropping the gun, pooping my pants, and making a run for it. By the end of the day, I would be covered with a warm fur coat and the bruin would go away with a full stomach. Some conservationists would call that a win, win.

"What's the closest you ever shot one?" I asked.

"I dropped one at less than ten feet. Thought he was goin' to skid slap bang into me. Another time I was salmon fishin' and bumped into an old sow, face to face. I slapped her nose as hard as I could with my pole and yelled 'get out of here!' Bears hate gettin' hit in the nose. I was lucky there were no cubs around. The main thing is to keep your wits. If you're afraid, you're done."

I find it hard to sleep the night before a major hunting or fishing trip. That night was no different. Every time I drifted off I had visions of skulls leering at me with big red eyes and bloody teeth. Again and again I dreamed of aiming my rifle at a grizzly crashing through the brush, always waking up before pulling the trigger. What a relief when morning came.

Nothing starts a good mountain morning like steak, eggs, and biscuits covered in rich milk gravy. After breakfast I headed to the barn. Nick kept an exceptionally well-trained string of saddle and pack horses. Bingo, a big roan, was the best of the bunch. He was reserved for Mac. Liam was given a spunky little pinto named Comanche, and I was "saddled" with Dusty. He gave me a dirty look and then puffed up his chest while I cinched up the saddle. I had never hunted from horseback. Nick showed me the proper way to secure my rifle scabbard. It was just the opposite of what I'd seen in cowboy movies. The rifle sits under your left leg with the butt at the front shoulder of the horse. You have to dismount before you can draw it out.

Nick explained, "You never shoot from the saddle! If you happen to aim near or between a horse's ears the pressure will blow out its eardrums. When we come up to a moose, step off and drop a rein. Dusty is trained to stay wherever you drop it. Then draw out your rifle and step away for the shot. And make sure it's a good shot. There's no need to track a wounded animal halfway from here to the Pacific. I'll be with you, but this is your hunt."

We packed our gear and returned to the house for coffee before hitting the trail. As soon as I was out of sight Dusty let out his breath. *Lesson to self: always give the cinch an extra pull after the horse has had a few minutes to deflate.* I had drunk about half a cup of coffee when Lucille stormed through the back door, planted both feet behind my chair, and glared down.

"Don't you know nuthin'!?"

Pastors aren't used to being yelled at, and certainly not by a woman, though some pastors' wives might surprise you. I noticed a smirk on Liam's face, and I swear Mac was bouncing up and down trying to stifle a snicker.

"How could you be so stupid as to leave your rifle in the scabbard and come into the house? I think you better go check your horse!"

I was flabbergasted. I changed color, though I don't remember if I went crimson from embarrassment or pale from fear. I stood up and walked to the corral. There was my beautiful .270 buried in mud and manure. And there was Dusty with a dumb expression, as if to say, "Don't look at me. I don't know what happened. Sorry I peed on your rifle." The rifle weighed about seven pounds, just enough to offset the weight of the saddle. Every time Dusty had shifted his weight, the saddle had slid a little to the rifle side. It was hanging upside down from his belly when I got there. Given enough time, he'd have stepped out of it and begun working on the bridle. He was one smart horse, and I was one sad hunter.

IT TOOK THE better part of the day to reach Nick's cabin. I hadn't been impressed by Dusty's performance at the ranch and I was downright depressed with his mule headed stubbornness on the trail. I've had a few horses in my time. They'd all had a competitive streak and fought to be first. If not reined in they were soon racing across the plain or through the brush. Not Dusty. He immediately dropped to the very rear. I think he figured that if the lead horse ran into a bear, we would have the advantage of being out front in getting away. For me, the rear meant eating dust and smelling horse apples and gee-gee farts for five or six hours. Without my constant encouragement Dusty would have turned and headed home. I have to admit, I dismounted and walked a few times. After a couple hours in the saddle I had what felt like a massive toothache in each knee. Ten years of driving around a church community doesn't prepare you for a trip by horseback.

A trapper had originally built the cabin. It was a mix of logs and rough-hewn lumber. Nick had added a lean-to that served as a porch for firewood and storage. There was a corral for the horses, a small shed for hay and tack, and a fifty-five-gallon drum of gasoline for a generator. Two pines about thirty yards from the cabin supported a long horizontal pole for hanging game. I've preached a number of sermons about the hereafter, but for a hunter, this was paradise.

Liam and I looked after the horses while Mac chopped wood and Nick lit the stove and put away supplies. We soon sat around a roughhewn table having fried chops and potatoes. After a quick clean-up, the hunting prep turned serious. Rifles, ammunition, knives, matches, socks, and boots were checked and set out for an early morning departure. My rifle required a good cleaning. Each of us wrapped several rounds of black electrical tape around the barrels of our rifles. A half inch or so was torn off and placed over the muzzle. The object was to keep debris and snow from falling into the barrel when walking through brush and trees. When shooting, the pressure blows the tape off with no effect on accuracy. We greased the outside of the barrels and stocks for protection from the damp but not the bolts and actions.

The cold will thicken any grease or oil on the mechanisms and make it hard to eject and load bullets. I normally keep my firearm inside when hunting, but not on this hunt. The rifles were left on the porch so there would be no sweating on the barrels from the heat of the cabin.

Bullet pouches, belts, knives, and other accessories were checked and double checked. I spent time admiring my knew Buck knife. It had two blades: one for cutting and the other for sawing. I had gone with the pocket version, but I still have a bit of nostalgia about my dad's old Bowie. As I sharpened and honed my knife I told the guys about my dad.

"You know," I said. "When my dad worked in the abattoir in Payette, Idaho where I grew up, he mastered the art of knife sharpening. He could spit on his arm and shave the hair with any knife on his work belt. In twenty years of trying I have yet to get an edge that sharp."

Nick politely listened the way guides do and then said, "Let me see your knife." He spit on his arm and with one swipe shaved off a two-inch strip of hair. "Maybe you need to learn how to shave."

After the chores were finished we settled into what became a nightly ritual – hot buttered rum. It guarantees a deep sleep and sweet dreams. Four bunks, two on each of the outer walls, awaited. I took an upper bunk. I had brought two sleeping bags, one inserted into the other, and a wool blanket. Once the fire burned out, the temperature would drop well below zero. We caught up with news of each other's families for a while. Then I read a book until the fuel ran out in the generator and the lights went out. Five hours later it was time to hit the trail.

THE HORSES SNORTED and stamped the frozen ground. Steam rose from their coats. Frost ringed their muzzles where their moist breath met the cold. We mounted and followed a mountain trail up and up and up. As we topped the tree line the sun greeted us on the eastern horizon. Orbs of light, called sun dogs, reflected from the frosty air on either side of the sun. An endless line of mountain peaks, all adorned with snow and ice, stretched across the horizon. Two miles away a large animal appeared as a tiny speck crossing a barren shoulder of rock. Nick dropped back to join me.

"That's a woodland caribou," he said. "They're a cousin of the reindeer in Finland. There used to be thousands of them. You don't see many these days. Overhunting and disruption of habitat is taking its toll. The big five trophies in North America are the black bear, the cougar, the moose, the grizzly, and the bison. Cougars are the most dangerous. They're quiet, quick, and canny. There's a debate about whether a true sportsman goes after the big five. If a guy just wants the coat or the head, that's fine by me. I can always find someone who needs the meat."

When the trail dropped back into the trees we split into two groups. Mac and Liam had been on several trips with Nick, so they could fend for themselves. Nick would ensure that I get my first moose. Within forty-five minutes we came across fresh tracks. Fifteen minutes later Nick pulled up and held a finger to his lips. We quietly dismounted and followed the tracks for about thirty yards.

"There's your moose," he whispered.

I had shot many deer but never a moose. From what I had read, a shot into the hump just above the shoulder will hit the spine and "good night" Mr. Moose. I took careful aim and shot through the tuft of hair on that hump. The moose trotted away; and I momentarily lost my mind. I started running after him through two or three feet of snow. Suddenly everything went white, then black, as I fell into a tree well. I had just managed to get onto my knees when I felt a strong hand under each armpit. Nick picked me up, turned me about twenty degrees, and set me on my feet.

"If you look close," he whispered, "you can see him standin' between those two trees."

I still have the antlers from that moose. They only span about twenty inches and look like two large cake spatulas. They could easily have graced the helmet of some Viking. I've carried them from British Columbia to Newfoundland and back again. They're one of the few things I'll eventually take to the home for old men. I look at them and can remember the entire "once upon a time" when I shot my first moose. Truth be told, it's the only moose I ever shot.

Walking back to the horses, we found fresh grizzly tracks crossing our footprints.

Nick bumped me on the shoulder, "We'll come back for the moose. Let's see where this fellow's goin'."

The tracks led through the trees, up and over a small spur jutting from the side of the mountain, and into a narrow ravine. They disappeared into the mouth of a small cave.

Nick grinned, "We got him! Now let's get Liam and Mac. I've been takin' Mac out for years and would like to see him bag a grizzly. There's plenty of daylight left for dressin' moose."

We returned to the horses and backtracked, looking for the other hunters. Within minutes Comanche and Bingo nickered a greeting to Dusty. The two horses were tethered to a ponderosa pine. Two sets of boot prints cut through the brush. *Boom!* Mac had just downed a moose. As Nick walked up to him, Mac pointed to a second bull emerging from a thicket far below.

Nick gave a nod. "Take him."

Boom! Mac was a shooter who never missed, never used more than one bullet, and always hit the heart. Everyone would take home meat.

"Get your horses," Nick commanded. "We'll be back. We've got some bear huntin' to do."

Things looked good, very good. The two sides of the ravine joined where the bruin's den entered a rocky outcropping. Just one set of tracks going in and none coming out. Mr. Bear would soon have a rude awakening. Nick stationed Mac about forty-five yards directly to the front of the cave. Liam and I sat on the hillside flanking the den. The scenario was perfect. Our instructions were clear, "If the grizzly doesn't drop on Mac's first shot, it's up to you to bring him down. Even a lethal shot doesn't always stop these big boys. Be alert and be ready."

Once everyone was in position, Nick crept to one side of the cave entrance. "Come out of there, you dirty *#*@#$%!" I can't repeat some of the language, but it was obvious that he questioned the parentage of that bear. Liam and I had our eyes glued on the cave. Our rifles were up and chambered and the safeties were off. Neither of us wanted to be blamed for losing a college chancellor.

"You hear that?" whispered Liam. "There's something in the brush behind us."

"Probably your imagination. Maybe a grouse or a rabbit. We'll check later. That bear's coming out any second."

We waited and waited and waited. Nick screamed into that dark hole. He threw rocks into it. He yelled. Nothing. He shrugged at Mac and spread his arms. "There must be a back door. Keep your wits and let's circle around."

It didn't take long to find a second cave entrance. The bruin had exited the rear of the den and ambled in a broad circle that led to a bluff about twenty yards behind me and Liam. At some point it tired of watching our foolishness and sauntered off into the woods. *Thank you Jesus!*

We rode back to a clearing near the first moose. Nick had packed sandwiches for everyone – finely ground meat, cooked and thickly spread on large slices of ranch-baked bread. These had been stuffed into a large coffee can. The tin was equipped with a makeshift handle of baling wire that attached through two nail holes at the open end. The emptied can soon hung over a crackling fire – and not one of those little two-match blazes we lit as boy scouts. Only a bonfire will keep people warm at minus fifteen degrees. My job was melting snow to boil coffee. As soon as the water bubbled and rolled with steam, Nick poured in a generous scoop of ground coffee. Smoke wrapped around the can, adding a flavor not found in any coffee shop, and a heavenly aroma wafted through the crisp mountain air. Several heaping tablespoons of sugar were added to the pot. After five minutes the can was removed from the fire and a large spoonful of fresh snow was tossed in. The snow gives the coffee a bit of a down flow that takes the grounds to the bottom. I've never had coffee like what we drank in the wilderness of the Chilcotin mountains.

An interesting observation about hunting. The fun lasts until you pull the trigger, then the work begins. It took the four of us to maneuver each moose into position for proper field dressing. After the animals were gutted, Nick stood spread-eagled over each moose and carefully split the neck and backbone from one end to the other with a short-handled axe. Soon the four quarters of each animal were covered with brush to discourage predators. We would return the following morning with the pack horses. Livers, hearts, and tongues were slung into the saddlebags. Such organs make great sandwich spreads.

I should mention that I once brought home a moose tongue. My wife, bless her heart, skinned and cooked it for me. She told me not to bother bringing another. I think the floppy old thing grossed her out. I'm of the opinion that if you peeled the skin off a tongue, tanned it, and added a zipper, it would make a dandy change purse. Can you imagine slapping that thing onto a store counter? My wife decidedly disagrees. I also brought home a deer brain once. I had heard that brains are good with scrambled eggs. It was kicked around our freezer for about six months before mysteriously disappearing. A small bear head I was saving went missing about the same time.

That evening Nick told us that if we had bagged the bear, it would have been his most successful day of hunting ever. We all agreed that it was time to celebrate. Nick broke out the rum and we settled down to a round of poker and storytelling.

Liam was chafed that Mac shot what he considered to be his moose. I didn't blame him. Hunting is not just about getting meat. You can do that at the grocery store. After a round of rum, Nick reminded Liam of his escapades over the years; like the year he and his brother rode horses at a full run across a meadow, hollering and firing pistols into the air. Liam just grinned. Seems he was somewhat flighty and had accidentally shot several cow moose over the years. *How hard can it be to recognize a set of moose horns?* Shooting an illegal animal can be costly. If caught, it means a hefty fine and loss of firearms. Some hunters leave the carcass for the bears, not taking any chances. Nick said he'd never waste such an animal. He would dress it, butcher it, and give it to one of the families in the area. Liam took the brunt of the evening and was given a good roasting. By the time we finished we were describing his "trophy" room as having one plaque after another of giant moose udders protruding from the wall.

Part of the recreational side of staying in a hunting camp is poker. I'm not a good gambler; I never win; and I get upset at losing. We played for matchsticks. Nick counted out twenty or thirty to each man and the game began. Before long I was "borrowing" from the "bank." Suddenly I was no longer having fun. The game had become a test of my male savvy. Standing only five-foot-six and weighing in at a hundred and forty, I sometimes battle with the Napoleon complex that plagues little men. I got so upset that I almost quit the game. Who knows what would have happened if we were playing for money. I mean, they weren't even my matchsticks. It's just the principle. Soon enough the gambling finished; we crawled into our sleeping bags; and the generator sputtered to a stop.

A packhorse can carry up to thirty percent of its own body weight, which for a thousand-pound horse means a load limit of 250 to 300 pounds. It took several trips to bring twelve quarters of meat down the mountain. Dusty, being a multi-talented horse, was drafted into packing. He took his normal position in last place, head to tail with the horse ahead. I followed on foot at a near trot. I soon had my head down in grim determination not to be left behind. Coming around a bend I ran smack into Dusty's tail. He turned his head back, lifted his upper lip in an equine sneer, and nearly suffocated me with a gee-gee fluffer-doodle.

The quarters made quite a sight hanging from the large pole secured between the pines; looked almost like an outdoor abattoir. Skinning was a chore. The hides had begun to freeze around the shanks and other areas close to the bone. It would have been easier if we had done it the previous day. Liam was still glum. He would have preferred to skin an animal he had personally bagged.

That night it was the normal round of hot-buttered rum followed by Fool's Poker. Fool's Poker is a game of bluff. Each player is dealt one or two cards which he holds to his forehead, face out. You don't see your own cards, but you see everyone else's. You bid based on what you see. Sounds dull as I put it to paper, but after a stiff mug of rum, it's a great game. Fellows point at each other laughing and carrying on like little boys. I'm not a good card player but I am a good bluffer and had found my game. Soon it was lights out. Just as I was getting deeper and deeper into the slumber of success, all hades broke loose in the horse coral. We heard stomping and snorting, planks splintering, and equine squeals of terror.

Nick sprang from his bunk. "It's a grizzly! Grab your guns. I'll get the flashlight!"

Can't you see it? Four men in long johns and heavy socks, one wearing an old tuque, all huddled together on the front stoop of a mountain cabin in the Canadian wilderness. Only a fool would venture more than two feet past the door. Liam and I were each on one knee with our rifles shouldered, locked, and loaded. Mac stood behind Liam, rifle ready. Nick stood behind me with a large flashlight.

"There he is!" shouted Nick.

Two large red eyes blinked from the dark. *BOOM! BOOM! BOOM!*

"Now he's over there!" *KAPOW! BLAM!*

"Hold the light still!"

"Heck! There's another one." *BOOM!*

An eerie silence followed.

"Did we get him?" whispered Liam. "Did we get him?"

Nick moved the light from left to right. The ghostly eyes of four horses stared at us from the corral. The bears were gone and there was no way to know if we had hit one.

Nick clicked off the flashlight. "Back to bed. No one's goin' out till mornin'. This is not a game. Things are gettin' dangerous. We need some good daylight before takin' a look."

I didn't sleep much after that and there was no familiar snoring coming from the other bunks. Come morning we had a mess of eggs, bacon, fried potatoes, and toast. When the sun was high enough for good light, we went out literally "loaded for bear." The horses were accounted for; no damage done except for a couple shattered planks on the corral. I didn't realize the "love-hate" relationship between bears and horses. Bears *love* horses. And horses *hate* bears, so much so that a horse will warn you about a bear's presence long before the family dog. Nick determined there had been not one, not two, nor even three, but four bears in the yard that night. One had been hit, leaving a small pool of frozen blood beside the corral and the occasional splash of blood in tracks going through the brush. The sides of meat had spared the horses. Huge claw marks were etched down the length of a front quarter on my moose where the ribs were partially ripped away from the backbone. Tracks were everywhere.

Now the real hunting began. We saddled the horses and Nick led the way. The first hour was easy. Tracks led up the trail where we had come down the day before. Occasionally Nick stopped for a closer look. The blood splashes were getting smaller and smaller. Then the tracks turned from the trail and led through the trees. We rode on until the blood sign ceased where the bear had entered into heavy underbrush. Nick pulled up his horse and turned, "This is gettin' too risky. If he's waitin', he'll be on us before we see him. Let's head back to camp. I'll radio Lucille and have her bring the dogs. We'll get an early start tomorrow. Unless there's another snowfall, he won't be hard to follow."

The cabin beckoned like a four-star hotel. Soon we sat before a hot fire. Inch thick steaks of beef, paired with fried potatoes and covered with thick gravy, graced the worn table. Nick checked his watch.

"Lucille will be done with chores and have the baby down by now. Good time to report in." He picked up the mic to a CB radio and flicked the on button.

"Breaker. Breaker. White Dove, come in. Breaker. This is Blowfly callin' White Dove. Come in White Dove."

"White Dove here. Read you loud and clear. What's happenin' at the Bullet Bin? Everyone okay?"

"White Dove, I need my heart pills." *Heart pills! I hope he's okay. Maybe we should just get him to a doctor.* "Bring the one's with the red label...and the dispenser. You know what I need. Oh, and have a couple nurses on call."

"Got you covered, Blowfly. See you at dawn. 10-4."

"Love ya. Over and out."

My heart sank as Nick hung up the mic. "Nick, you got a heart problem?" I asked. "We can go home early."

He shook his head and winked, "I don't have a heart problem, but I know a flea-bitten bruin that's likely to have heart failure tomorrow. I asked Lucille to bring my 44 Magnum and a box of shells. Better for anyone listenin' to think I have a heart condition than to know we're grizzly huntin'. Those that know me, know better. And those that don't, wonder why I'm still alive. The dogs, Lucky and Ginger, are the best nurses around for takin' care of a wounded bear."

There was a good chance of more company that night. We had close to fifteen hundred pounds of meat hanging outside, and I'm not the sharing type. I decided to build a large fire to keep the bears away from our meat. I left the cabin, flashlight in one hand, axe and rifle in the other. Every few feet I shined the light in a large arch. I didn't want to get ambushed. I walked about fifteen yards and slowly shined the light from side to side. Two ginormous blood-red eyes stared out from the trees. Well, the axe got tangled up in my rifle sling and I dropped the flashlight. Probably a good thing. I was so scared I would have shot an old skidoo right between the two rear reflectors. Why Nick had parked it there was beyond my understanding. Thankfully no one witnessed my consternation. Later that night I snuck out and changed into my spare set of thermals. The old ones had acquired a large smelly brown patch in the seat. There would be no outdoor fire that night, bears or no bears.

We were finishing clean-up from breakfast the following morning when we heard the clip-clop of a horse and the squeak of wagon springs. Lucky and Ginger bounded to the cabin, tails wagging. Lucky was a large shepherd cross with a brindle grey, black, and white coat. Ginger was slightly smaller with the speckled brown coat and yellow eyes you'd expect in an Australian cattle dog. Lucille was all smiles. Baby Ciara reached toward Nick with both arms from the safety of a warm snuggly. Lucille had loaded a few extra supplies plus Nick's pistol and ammo. As Nick and Lucille exchanged the latest news from the ranch, Liam and I loaded the front quarters of our moose onto the wagon. The rear quarters would be packed out with the horses. Lucille had coffee and then headed down the mountain, needing to get back by mid-morning for the regular ranch chores.

Nick gave some final instructions before we mounted. "We have to be on our toes. When the dogs catch up with the bear, he'll stop to fight. Don't get too close and make sure you have a good shot. I don't want to lose a dog. If the dogs get confused and pick up the wrong scent, we could have a serious problem. Normally a grizzly will circle back to see what's following him. Terry, you'll be in the rear, so don't go to sleep." *Sleep? You've got to be kidding. I'll bet this is Dusty's fault!*

Dusty was quite content to pull drag. Maybe it was his way of getting rid of me. He would sense a grizzly long before I would, could buck me off, and wish me well. I can almost read the thoughts of some bear coming from behind, "*Dusty or Terry? Flank steak or rump roast? Hmm.*"

I'm reminded of the fellow who surprised a sow and two cubs while picking huckleberries. He dropped his bucket and was hightailing it down the mountainside. He should have known that you'll never outrun a grizzly. Like any outdoorsman in trouble, he suddenly became very religious, "O God, if you just get me out of this one, I promise..." Running out of wind, he stumbled and fell. All was suddenly quiet. Rolling over, he saw that the bear had stopped about ten feet behind him. "I've been s-s-saved," he stuttered. "Praise the Lord, I've been saved!" Momma bear stood there waiting for the cubs to catch up. Then all three knelt down. The last thing the berry picker heard was, "Thank you, Lord, for the food we are about to receive."

Back to Dusty. As we rode through the trees he took me under every low limb he could find and leaned into every passing tree trunk. My face was scratched, my pants were shredded, and my legs were black and blue. *Lesson to self: one hundred percent virgin wool suit trousers are not designed for hunting*. Anytime I dismounted, Dusty feigned an affectionate look and flapped his eyelids at me. The worst part was the embarrassment. No one else had shredded pants, bruised knees, and facial scratches.

Late in the day we reached a clearing where Lucky and Ginger had caught up with the bruin. There was evidence of a skirmish, but the grizzly had brushed the dogs aside and moved on, intent on reaching the other side of the mountain. Just *to see what he could see*, I suppose. Why else would a bear go *over the mountain*? The bear was gone, the dogs were gone, and the day would soon be gone. We reconnoitered around Nick.

"We'll have to let him go. We can't chance bein' caught in the dark. Just too dangerous. We best get back 'cause we'll likely have more company tonight."

It was dusky when we rode up to the cabin. Liam and I took the horses to the corral to give them a well-deserved bucket of oats and a slice of hay. Nick was getting the generator going. Mac was starting the fire. And there it was, a silver-tip grizzly sauntering into camp. Liam and I grabbed our rifles. He fired and the bear dropped just out of sight on the opposite side of an ice-covered creek. I was hyped and was about to run toward the spot when a firm hand grasped my shoulder.

"Where do ya think ya're goin'?" It was Nick. "He may be down, but that doesn't mean he's dead, and it's almost dark. We'll look in the mornin'. I've never lost a hunter and I don't plan to now."

As we sat down to supper there was scratching at the door. Mac opened it and there was Lucky. He flopped onto the floor, tongue lolling out and tail slowly wagging. He had four massive claw marks across his back and was missing a large patch of skin on one shoulder. "Lucky Dog" took on a new meaning that night.

Nick gave the pooch an affectionate pat. "Well, boy, looks like ya gave it your best. Ya won't need stitches, but we'll put some salve on those wounds. Where's your buddy?" He turned to Mac, "Darn! Those dogs always stick together. Ginger was Lucille's favorite. How do I tell her we lost her dog?"

Everyone was quiet as we sipped our hot-buttered rum. I don't normally pray for animals, but that night I put in a few words for Ginger. *Lord, if there's any possible way to bring back that dog.... I mean, these people have been so good to me.... Well, you know what I mean. Before Ciara, Ginger was Lucille's baby. Please, please, please. This trip has been so good, but it won't be the same if we've lost that woman's dog.*

Around two in the morning the horses began snorting and tramping around the coral. Everyone was immediately awake and climbing out of their bunks.

Nick whispered, "Slow down guys. We've got a wolf or coyote prowlin' around."

How does he do that? This guy even understands horse talk.

Lucky gave out a friendly yip and we heard a whine at the door. Ginger was back. *Thank you, Lord!* She was tuckered out and her winter coat was covered in burrs, but she wasn't beat up like Lucky. We were happy to see her, and her tail wag left no doubt that she was happy to see us.

The next morning we found a large pool of blood where Liam's bruin had dropped but no bear. We saddled up and followed a blood trail for about three quarters of a mile before coming to a beautiful silver-tipped grizzly curled up beneath an overhang along the creek.

"Congratulations Liam," said Nick. "Ya got your bear. Ya shot him. Now ya skin him."

I had heard that bears are Nature's garbage can. Like their relative, the pig, they'll eat almost anything, the rottener, the better. When Liam opened the grizzly the stench was overbearing. Whatever it had been eating was fermenting in its gut. Liam started retching and then vomited into a nearby bush. For the next hour intermittent gagging and heaving brought rounds of laughter from the rest of us. We thought that was so funny. It's been over thirty years since that trip, and I still laugh at Liam's antics. *Lesson to self: don't do something embarrassing in front of your buddies unless you want to hear about it for the rest of your life.*

While Liam looked after the bear, Mac and I returned to the cabin to retrieve the pack horses and load gear for the ride back to the ranch. The bear hide meant that we were short one pack horse. Since Liam shot the bruin, we voted three to one that he could hoof it. But his horse was not having anything to do with a grizzly, dead or alive. When approached with the bear hide, Comanche bucked and reared and snorted, nearly ripping the sapling he was tied to out of the ground.

Dusty was next in line for packing the pelt. He showed no fear. I'm convinced his olfactory senses had been destroyed from his preferred position at the rear of the herd. This time we pulled straws to see who would walk. I pulled the short straw. With my height, I always seem to get the *short* end of things. At first I led Dusty, but he was in a rush to get back to the warm stall, rolled oats, and fresh hay of the ranch barn. Going up the mountain he had to be coaxed and cajoled every step of the way but not going down. I was soon hanging onto his tail for fear of being left behind. Everyone else made a rush to be first for a hot bath, a home-cooked meal, and a warm bed. Somehow they forgot about our agreement to take turns walking.

The following morning we loaded Liam's van and had one last coffee before hitting the road. I took a final stroll, more like a hobble, to the barn. I admire people who carve a homestead out of the wilderness. Nick and Lucille grew their own vegetables, picked wild berries and fruit, and raised their own meat. Lucille knew all the wild plants and native medicines. Nick was self-sufficient as a blacksmith and mechanic. They lived on the land and lived off the land. I heard a nicker and Dusty put his head over the top rail of the corral. He batted his big eyelids at me and nudged my breast pocket with his velvety nose as if to say, "Any apple slices or sugar lumps in there? Let's be friends." I scratched between his ears and patted his neck. *You're okay for a horse, but next time I'll take Comanche.*

OLE THE SWEDE

ONE THING ABOUT being in the "bush," you soon meet people who *are* "bushed." I often wonder if they were crazy before they moved into the wilderness or became crazy after. Whatever, crazy is crazy. Ole Olsen is a case in point. Ole claimed he came from Sweden, though his name was Danish. Guess those Danes got around. Anyway, Ole offered to take me and my buddy, Russel, hunting. We drove Russel's '72 Volkswagen Beetle through bush and snow to Ole's cabin. Without the rear engine and sixteen-inch tires we never would have made it. German engineers knew what they were doing when they designed the Beetle. Ole had promised, "You come see Ole, you soon have your deer, believe you me. Just you wait.".

That afternoon Ole posted Russ and me on opposite sides of a ravine.

"The deer, he come between you, you see," he promised. "I go now to see what he be doing. Will come back soon." With that, Ole disappeared over the ridge.

The first hour was all anticipation but no deer. My butt began to numb from sitting on a granite outcropping, so I paced in place for a while. No deer. I ate a peanut butter sandwich. No deer. Sat some more and poured a coffee from my thermos. No deer. I hate posting for game, whether it's on a ridge or in a tree stand or just sitting in my car. I like walking and stalking. Sitting and waiting is so boring.

As the sun dropped lower and lower, the temperature grew colder and colder. No deer and no Ole. A cold wind blew into my face. I pulled my jacket over my mouth and nose. It was cold! My glasses fogged. My hands numbed. I held the rifle with one hand and tried to warm the other under an armpit. As I shivered in the cold I began my hunting mantra, "I'm having fun...I'm having fun...I'm having...." I tried chanting it to the tune of "I Found My Thrill on Blueberry Hill," and finally changed the words to "I am so cold...I am so cold..."

The sun went behind a mountain. Still, no deer and no Ole. It was time to cross the ravine and talk Russ into returning to the cabin. Not finding Ole at the cabin, we began to worry. Ole knew the area like the back of his hand – or was it the small of his back? Surely, he couldn't be lost. It was too late to go looking, so we left a lantern in the window and went to bed. Next morning we were up before daylight. If we hit the trail before the morning sun melted the snow we might get lucky and come across his tracks.

We had just closed the cabin door when a mournful cry echoed down the valley, "Ole the Swede, lost on the mountain. Anybody find me, I give him five dollars!"

Russ looked at me, "I think he's lost his marbles. Even I could find my way to this cabin."

Up the mountain we went.

"Ole the Swede, lost on the mountain. Anybody find me, I give him five dollars!"

If we followed the sound, we were bound to find Ole. The problem: Ole kept moving around. It took us about two hours before coming across him in a small clearing near a mountain spring.

"Ole! Are you alright?" I said. "We're here for you buddy."

Ole turned with a look of fear and horror. He raised his rifle and started shooting. I hit the dust, my years of pretending to be a soldier as a kid finally being put to good use. Ole turned and charged into the brush shouting, "You never get Ole Olsen!"

Russ peeked from behind a tree, "Now I'm sure the old fella's a brick short. I've heard of guys getting paranoid in the later stages of hypothermia but it ain't that cold."

Soon we heard him from about two hundred yards away. "Ole the Swede. Lost on the mountain. Anybody find me, I give him five dollars." We snuck up on him again. This time a bullet creased my hat and once again Ole fled into the trees. "You never get Ole Olsen!" Fifteen minutes later, "Ole the Swede. Lost on the Mountain. Anybody find me, I give him five dollars!"

We needed help, so we trekked back to the cabin. As luck would have it, a couple of Ole's friends had driven in for an afternoon of rabbit hunting. I was already uncertain of Ole's sanity and soon had similar doubts about his buddies. Seems that "bushed" people have "bushed" buddies. The fellows were intent on saving him but short on brains.

Clem Chisel figured we should set out some bear traps. "A steel trap can do a lot of damage," he said, "but six or eight weeks in a good cast and Ole will be good as new."

Newt Newton thought a covered pit would be better. Clem disagreed. A pit would only work if we knew where Ole was, and which trail he would take. For certain, we didn't want him running after us with a .30-30. Other ideas included a snare, a net, wounding him in the leg, and waiting until he was half frozen. The issue with every plan was knowing where the old codger was hiding and avoiding that .30-30.

Newt's wife, Elvira, came up with an idea that was thought to be foolproof. The boys took apart an old camp stove, one of those that's used for tents in the winter. They loaded a mule named Buckeye with the fire box, legs, stove pipe, and oven. Elvira followed with flour, pans, and huckleberries. They found the clearing where we'd last heard Ole. Newt and Clem set up the stove and Elvira went to work. Soon the aroma of fresh perked coffee wafted up the mountainside. The indescribable smell of warm huckleberry pie seeped through the pines. Elvira spread a cloth over a large stump and set everything out restaurant style. Then everyone hid in the brush. Within minutes we heard the rustle of branches and the soft tread of boots in the undergrowth. Ole's head appeared from a thicket. His eyes bulged and rolled from side to side like an old toad eyeing a grasshopper. Several days of grey stubble covered his chin. He slowly worked his way toward the stump, carefully looking around the clearing.

When you're crazy, a stump in the middle of the wilderness covered with a tablecloth and set with a steaming cup of coffee, a large slice of huckleberry pie, and a fresh pitcher of cream seems like the most natural thing in the world. Ole sat cross legged, peered around once more, and set down the rifle. He pulled a dirty red bandanna from his pocket and tucked it into his shirt below his chin. As he brought a large bite of pie to his mouth, Clem and Newt sprung. Ole was determined they'd never take him and fought like a momma bear protecting her cubs. Finally, Elvira jumped into the fray and knocked Ole out with a frying pan. The guys tied his hands and feet and wrapped so much rope around him that he looked like a mummy. Then they finished off the pie and drank the coffee. No point in letting it go to waste. Next, they draped Ole over Buckeye and began the trip down the mountain.

I don't know what finally happened to the Swede but the last time I visited Williams Lake I heard a strange voice coming from the top floor of the Cariboo Memorial Hospital. "Ole the Swede. Lost on the mountain. Anybody find me, I give him five dollars!"

MAKE UP YOUR MIND

MY SONS, MIKE and Sean, didn't take to fishing but I fantasized about hunting with the boys. I envisioned setting up camp and sitting around a campfire with a couple nice bucks hanging from a nearby tree. That turned out about as successful as when I brought home a drum set with dreams of a family band. Some things can't be forced.

As soon as Mike turned fourteen he passed the hunter safety requirements and acquired his first hunting license. I immediately added a 20-gauge shotgun to my gun cabinet and purchased a pellet gun for Sean who was several years younger. That fall we hit the woods. My wife, Lin, packed a lunch and two thermoses. We donned our jackets, hats, and boots, and drove to the wilderness for some grouse hunting. A couple notes about Lin. She's the most enthusiastic supporter any hunter could ever dream of having. She's never shot anything, and I'll have to see her do it to believe she can. She told me that she didn't mind that I shot the occasional fools hen, but she was dead set against duck hunting. According to her, ducks mate for life and it's a terrible sin to break up a marriage; not to mention that she's not crazy about the taste of the mud ducks I bring home. Even though she loves venison, I can't see her ever shooting a deer. When a likely freezer candidate steps forth from the brush, Lin sees Bambi. I see a meat chart. We're a great combination!

Back to that first family hunt. Initially a moderate rain confined us to the car. As the clouds lifted, the birds came out of the underbrush and we emerged from our vehicle. We quietly worked our way down an old bush road. Mike spotted two fools hens just as they strutted behind a large spruce.

"Did you see those, Dad?" He whispered.

I held out a hand signaling everyone to stop and then put one finger to my lips for silence. I pointed at Mike and whispered, "When they come out, you shoot the one on the left and I'll take the one on the right."

We waited, guns ready. *BLAM!* Mike fired before I saw anything. I quickly shouldered my 12-gauge. No birds emerged. He had nailed both grouse with one shot. In fifty-five years of hunting I've never managed to do that. I was some proud!

Deer season arrived and I added a bolt action Savage .30-30 to my rifle collection. We were new to Kamloops so a couple fellows I met at church offered to drive Mike and me to a forested area northwest of the city. It was a perfect day. Fresh snow revealed dozens of deer tracks. Does of all sizes peeked from the trees, but we needed a buck. We walked and we drove, and we drove and we walked, but no bucks. At the last glimmer of daylight three deer stepped onto the road about a hundred yards in front of the car.

"There's your buck, son," I said.

Everyone piled out. Mike got on one knee, leaned against the car, and lined up his shot.

A guy named Will exclaimed, "Don't shoot! That's not a buck!"

"Yes it is," I said.

"No it's not."

"Yes it is."

"No it's not."

An exasperated teenager interrupted. "Will you guys make up your mind?"

I turned and said, "Shoot!"

He did and bagged the nicest little two-point buck you ever saw. But even with this initial success, Mike didn't take to hunting. He enjoyed going so long as I let him drive on the bush roads. He loved camping and became a great outdoorsman, but he didn't like killing such beautiful creatures. I suspect an infamous duck hunt pounded the final nail into his hunting coffin.

I had purchased an old VW Westfalia as a family project. Mike and I were traveling to the Lumby area for a weekend of whitetail hunting. Enroute we stopped for some duck hunting with a friend in Enderby. The fellow, Chuck was his name, shot a mallard which fell slap dab in the middle of a pond. Chuck wouldn't retrieve it, so I took what was becoming my annual autumn swim. *O how nice it would be to have a dog.* Chuck didn't want the bird. He said his wife wouldn't cook it and his kids wouldn't eat it. *So why go hunting?*

Join a gun club for your fun and leave the wildlife alone. I tossed the duck into the back of our van, thinking we would have it for supper.

We pulled into a station in Vernon for gas. I was at the pumps and Mike was sitting in the vehicle when Mr. Duck came back to life. He didn't just quack or move a wing; the dang thing went berserk. It flew into the windshield, then retreated toward the rear of the vehicle, banged into the sides, and was making noises never heard before and probably never heard since. Mike was frantically trying to catch it. I was squeezing tighter on the fuel nozzle, hoping to get out of there before being arrested for transporting a live wild animal. It was like the duck was demon possessed. Stephen King would be hard pressed to write such a terrible scenario. Poor Mike. With multiple scratches and a valiant effort at neck wringing, he finally silenced the ill-fated bird. If it hadn't already been wounded, we would have simply released it out the back door. We finished our weekend and brought home a nice little spike buck, but that trip killed Mike's enthusiasm for hunting.

AND THEN THERE was Sean. Whereas Mike was up and ready any time of day, Sean wasn't an early riser. I would drag him from bed in what must have seemed like the middle of the night with a "Come on Sean. We're going hunting." What that really meant was, "I'm going hunting and you get to be my sidekick." He was a good sport and a willing companion, just not so early in the morning. I'll never forget the day I roused him out around 5:00 and headed for the hills. By 6:00 we were wending up a logging road. I soon had to pull over and let him do a good upchuck in the ditch. Early mornings and winding roads were not his cup of tea. *What kind of dad does that to his kid?*

Whenever we joined a group hunt, Sean always teamed up with me, somewhat like my first trips with his Grandpa Gary. On one of those trips we had bounced and rattled up a decommissioned road onto the Red Plateau above Kamloops Lake. The deer had been in the rut for about a week, a good time to get a buck. During the breeding season male mulies follow the does around like lovesick puppies tailing behind their mommas. All sense of danger and caution goes to the wind. There's only one thing on a buck's mind, and you can guess what that is.

Fresh snow covered the ground, which meant that any tracks we came across would be no older than the early morning. Sean and I left the car and trekked down the road looking for a suitable spot to cut into the woods. We had gone twenty yards when I spotted two sets of fresh tracks.

"Look son. See this set of tracks. Those two spots at the back of each print are from dewclaws. This deer's heavier than the other one and most likely a buck. See, the other tracks are smaller and no dewclaw marks. That's his girlfriend. We'll follow these and see where they go."

Around thirty yards into the bush a little voice whispered from behind me, "Dad, use your deer call."

I pulled out my Deer Stopper, puckered up my lips and blew through the rubber bands. *Ma...ma...maaa.* Nothing. *Ma...ma...mama.* No response. *Ma...maaaa.*

It's hard work dogging behind your daddy when you could be home watching cartoons. In resignation, Sean flopped against the trunk of a tree and blew a raspberry, "*ppbbbt!*"

A loud *phoo* burst from the shrubs to the left of the trail. *Phoo!* That woke up both lad and dad. Sean's eyes were as big as saucers.

I held a finger to my lips and whispered, "You wait here while I sneak up to the turn in the trail. When I give you the signal, you slowly walk into the brush." *What was I thinking? Who asks his ten-year-old to do that?* I reached the bend and signaled. Sean crept into the undergrowth. A doe crossed the trail ahead of me followed by a nice big buck. One shot and down it went. I had Sean shoot what I call the insurance shot just behind one ear. That "insures" the deer isn't going jump back up and surprise me.

Sean was a fine little hunting companion. As soon as he was of age, I signed him up for a junior hunting license so he could carry the .410 in case we came across a grouse. One fall we encountered a wounded bear. Someone had shot and broken its left shoulder. The bruin was running along the side of the road with its injured leg flopping at its side. It cut into the woods before I could stop the car. That's one time I would have brought home bear for the freezer. I hate seeing anything suffer. Hunters should never take a bad shot!

Later that day we parked next to a duck pond. Sean hid in the willows on one side while I walked around the slough. The flock swam away from me and within shooting range of Sean. *Bang!* He bagged his first and only duck. He's not partial to wild fowl, and like his older brother, does not take to hunting. However, both sons, and now my grandsons, love camping and feel right at home in the wilderness. I can't think of a better legacy to give them than a wholehearted appreciation of nature.

"Will you guys make up your mind?"
These antlers grace the wall in my office.

Sean was a great companion, both field and stream.
I pickled these pike minnows.

CHELSEA

FROM THE DAY my dad gave me my first shotgun, a Marlin .410, I've spent hours following fence lines, wandering through fields, and exploring the woods for game birds. Clint McGregor, a neighbor of ours, had a hunting dog named Rusty.

Rusty was well trained. He would locate a pheasant in the brush, lift a front leg, and point his nose at the hidden prey. After the hunters were positioned, Clint would give a hand signal and Rusty would leap into the thicket. When a bird was shot, he retrieved and dropped it at Clint's feet with a big doggy grin that said, "Aren't I the greatest dog you ever saw?" If you happened to wound a pheasant and it took off running or hid in a corn patch, Rusty soon tracked it down.

On my way home from school one day, I stopped to say hello to Clint, hoping to be invited on an outing. Rusty ran up the drive to meet me, happy as lark. When Clint appeared, the pooch suddenly hung his head and limped up the steps of the front porch. He flopped down and stared mournfully at Clint.

Clint looked at him, “You cut that out, you old phony. There’s nothing wrong with you.”

“Is he hurt?” I asked.

“He’d like me to think so. Last time out he wouldn’t stay inside the shooting range and kept getting too far ahead. He wasn’t paying attention, so I peppered him with a little birdshot. Now every time I walk into the room, he makes like I nearly killed him. Just a little game we play.”

“You shot your own dog?”

“No damage done. Watch this.”

Clint walked to his den, Rusty keeping one eye on him each step of the way. When Clint returned with his 12-gauge, Rusty let out a joyous yelp and leapt to his feet. He was instantly at Clint’s side looking up with a look of adoration only a faithful dog can give. The limp was gone. All was forgiven.

THIRTY YEARS LATER I waited in a parking lot for a special delivery. I had purchased a Springer Spaniel from a breeder in Prince George, British Columbia. A trucker pulled up with a nine-week-old puppy tucked in a box on the passenger seat. Chelsea, a little black and white puppy, had never been away from her mother until hitching a ride to Kamloops. Initially she was afraid to go into the back yard, preferring to snuggle up to a black and white socker ball on the patio. I guess it reminded her of her brothers and sisters.

Right off the bat I picked up all the training equipment: collar, leash, whistle, retriever dummies.

As soon as she was old enough we enrolled in puppy training. Springers are a high energy dog but ours extended the energy needle to new heights. She came from a hunting line of forebears and could easily cover fifty miles a day. To get her settled for puppy class required an hour-long run in advance. Still, she was a challenge. At one point the instructor asked for the lead to my dog. She was going to "show me a thing or two" about how to control a puppy. A few minutes later she dragged Chelsea back, handed me the leash, and said, *"hyper"*. I had her commiseration after that. Chelsea was the most haywire dog you can imagine. She had high energy and long endurance, but her inner wiring was crossed.

I took Chelsea pheasant hunting when she was a little over six months old. Initially she was all nose but had no understanding as to what she was "nosing." Within thirty minutes she flushed two nice pheasant cocks. I winged one which tumbled to the ground and sprinted toward a hedgerow. *This is why I have a dog!*

"Fetch!" I cried.

I watched the pheasant disappear into the weeds. No dog appeared in pursuit. I looked around. No dog anywhere near. I looked again. Chelsea was half a field away chasing the other bird. Her thought must have been, *you get the runner while I chase the flier.* By the time I ran down the dog, the runner was gone.

I decided to try shooting a duck on a nearby irrigation pond. Dropped one right in the middle of the pond, a good shot if I do say. We had played hours of fetch in my backyard. I had taped duck wings to a dummy to make it as real as possible. Chelsea would retrieve it but made horrible faces and nearly gagged at the taste. The thought of swimming to fetch such an awful tasting thing had never entered her little puppy pea brain. I threw a stick out beside the duck. She ran as far as the water's edge and gave me an incredulous look. *If you want that stick, why are you throwing it into the pond?*

It was a cool day, but I refused to waste that duck. *Don't shoot what you can't eat and always retrieve what you shoot.* I stripped down to my skivvies and stepped into the water. *Brrr!* Soon I was doing the breaststroke to the center of the pond. I heard a splash and Chelsea paddled up beside me. She gave me a loving look. *So where are we going? This is fun.* She wasn't interested in the duck until I secured it in my left hand and began the side stroke with my right. Suddenly the pooch decided it was her duck. *This could be good.*

Six months is too young to start a pup in the field. By the end of the day she had sprained a hip. Bird season ended before I could take her out again, which meant a nine month wait before the next hunting season. In the meantime I frequented the shooting range to acclimatize her to the big "bang." She loved every minute. At the sight of the shotgun she would spring two feet into the air and dash for the truck. *Let's go!*

Please recall that I had been going to puppy training classes. Chelsea had the basic commands down pat. Sit. Heal. Fetch. Come. She obeyed perfectly; that is, in the house, in the backyard, or on a leash. Along the river or in the woods was different. As soon as she picked up a scent she took off. A dog's sense of smell is fifty times greater than a human's and the portion of its brain dedicated to odor analysis is forty times greater. Like other Springers, Chelsea had what's called neophilia, an attraction to new smells. I've got a feeling that my dog was a neophiliac because she was constantly taking off after one thing or another.

One time we came on a flock of fifty or sixty geese feeding along the South Thompson River. She charged into the middle of the flock. The geese scattered, regrouped, and landed about fifteen yards from shore. No problem. Chelsea leapt into the cold water and swam after them. The flock maintained about ten yards of separation and swam further. Chelsea paddled after them. I feared she would go too far and drown. Eventually she swam to shore with the flock following only five yards behind her. They played this game of swimming out and back half a dozen times. I gave up waiting and walked upriver, expecting the dog would eventually tire out and join me. I hadn't gone far when a familiar bark drew my attention to the middle of the river. The geese had divided into two clusters, both swimming upstream. Halfway between them was a little black and white spaniel happily paddling along like one of the flock.

I spent hours throwing a mock duck in the backyard and shouting, "fetch!" On the lead Chelsea was flawless. But unclipped, she developed a habit of running toward the dummy and then jumping over the fence at the scent of anything interesting, which included mice, rabbits, birds, the neighbor's cat, etc. Sometimes she didn't reappear for two hours. It seemed to me that I was becoming the retriever. *Maybe the real thing will be different.* Come duck season I drove to a large pond. I got out of the truck with the dog on a leash. We sat in the brush waiting. Three mallards soon drifted over the water. Chelsea didn't see them. *So far, so good.* Just before shooting, I unclipped the lead. BANG! Down came a duck. Chelsea sprang into action. She was in the water, out of the water, into the woods, and around the truck. She went absolutely mental, running everywhere except into the pond. I don't think she had even seen the duck. I calmed her down and pointed to the mallard. "Fetch!" She gave me a dumb look as though to say, "fetch what?" I threw a stick out beside the duck. She brought back the stick. After half a dozen throws, she noticed the duck. *At last!* She took the duck and started toward shore. "Good dog!" About halfway back she came across a stick, dropped the duck, and retrieved the stick.

I didn't want to take a swim. I waded till the cold muddy water was about to breach my waders and reached out with a long limb. The mud sucked at my feet. Water slowly dribbled into my left boot. I could barely touch the duck with the limb but couldn't quite snag it. Chelsea was watching with great interest. A lightbulb lit up in her little brain. She jumped into the water and swam to the duck. "Good dog!" She gently took the bird into her mouth. "Yes!" And then swam to the middle of the pond, dropped the duck, and brought back a stick. "Nooooo!" I had a conniption fit. I waived my arms and jumped up and down like a three-year old. "Fetch, you little twit!" Had anyone driven by, I would have been committed to the local psych ward.

Eventually I calmed down and sat on a log. Chelsea, sensing it was now safe to approach, trotted over and laid her muzzle on my knee. I gave her a pat. "Maybe ducks aren't your thing, girl. Let's head for the woods and see how you do with grouse."

She was smart in a dumb sort of way. If I zigzagged through the brush, she zigzagged through the brush. If I stayed on the trail, she stayed on the trail – just far enough ahead to ensure that I wouldn't get within shooting range of anything. I decided she must be a "Greenpeace" dog. I could almost read her mind as she sometimes bolted ahead. *Run! He's coming with a gun. Run for your lives*. She never did grasp the proper division of labor. She was a great companion and I loved taking her along but if I drove past a flock of grouse and wanted to bag one, I had to leave the dog in the truck.

On one occasion, we had been out all day. She was curled up on the passenger seat, wet, cold, and exhausted. I passed a covey of fools hens, pulled over and stepped out with the shotgun, quickly shutting the door so Chelsea couldn't follow. First, she whined. Then she howled and cried. It was downright embarrassing. I tried to block out the sound. I needed to bag at least one bird in order to maintain my manliness. I crept up the side of the road and took aim. The horn blasted from the truck. Birds flew in all directions. I fired and missed. That silly dog had gotten tangled up in the steering wheel while trying to dig her way through the door.

Rabbit hunting was no better. I was in a good area for rabbits and came across a poor little bunny that had been hit by a car. I stopped to introduce Chelsea to the scent. She showed no interest. If it didn't run or hop or fly, what was the point? My hopes of a dream dog were diminishing but "hope springs eternal." I parked the truck and entered the woods. Soon a snowshoe hare dashed across the trail. That got Chelsea's attention. What did she do? She started backtracking, probably thinking, *I wonder where he came from.*

I finally had to ask myself, "What's more important, getting a few extra grouse and ducks, or enjoying the great outdoors with a fun companion?" This took some mental adjustments. Chelsea was a doggy dingbat no matter what I did. Even fishing was a challenge. You may have seen footage of the wise hunter with his well-mannered Labrador retriever sitting at the bow of his boat. I bet you never saw one with a springer spaniel that had jumped overboard with her leash attached, dragging behind the boat like a drift anchor. So much for trolling. No worry. There are plenty of creeks and small lakes where I live.

Wentworth Creek is a tiny little creek about forty-five minutes out of Kamloops, British Columbia. I like to go there for fun about once a year. There's the odd rabbit and bear in the area. I thought it would be the perfect place to take the dog. She would get her run, and I would explore the odd hole where little brookies lurk. "Little" is the operative word. Eight inches is a big fish in that creek, but brookies are great fighters.

I hiked through willows, between spindly spruce, and across a velvety carpet of green moss and ginger-colored leaves to a beautiful pool. My faithful canine zigzagged through the undergrowth, nose to the ground. We reached a small clearing where water cascades over large granite boulders to a small pool of swirling, gurgling water. Mossy grey rocks line the bank and multi-colored gravel covers the bottom. I never fail to catch a couple fish from that hole, as least, not until that trip. As I flicked my line into the water, I saw a streak of black and white from my right. Chelsea made an Olympic leap into the middle of the pool. I can imagine her thoughts, *I'll get it, I'll get it!* as fish fled in all directions. Her head bobbed from the water frantically looking about as if to say, "Where'd it go?" Apart from the splash of my lure, I wonder if she even knew what "it" was.

So much for creek fishing. I returned to the truck and drove another fifteen miles to Whitewood Lake. I stopped at a protected campsite adjacent a gravelly beach. Chelsea could sniff and dig to her heart's delight, while I filled my creel with pan-size trout. Here I used the trick I learned in Newfoundland, only sliding a slip bobber up the line instead of using a piece of dowel. British Columbia allows only one hook, so I attached my favorite fly, a tiny green shrimp, to the leader. First cast. Flash of black and white. This time there was actually something to retrieve and fifteen yards of line to get tangled. *Dang!*

I loved that dog but give me a break. "Come!" I muttered. "We could have so much fun if only you would behave like a normal dog!" I tied her to a tree, untangled my line, and stepped back to the shore. A strange cooing and whining began, Chelsea's way of pleading for freedom. Howling and crying followed. I turned to see her chewing through the willow branch that held her lead. More pathetic cooing. Growling. A vicious attack at her leash.

"Okay, okay! Stop! You're killing me."

Back to the truck. I knew a good place for wild raspberries. Unfortunately a large black bear knew about the same spot. *Darn!* Chelsea froze in position and pointed with her right paw – miracle number one! Then she looked at me for a command – miracle number two! I could almost read her mind. *Please let me chase it. Please. Please. Please.* Field Springers are bred for fur *and* feather, and I think Chelsea would have made a great bear dog. She was not afraid of anything. Thankfully, this was one of the few times that she "heeled" – miracle number three – as we returned to the truck. I was hoping for miracles four, five, and so forth, but I guess miracles only come in threes. You have to be grateful for what you get.

Chelsea's greatest passion was to get a marmot. She tried ever so hard to stalk those crafty critters. Slowly moving a paw, then freezing, then moving the other paw, she'd creep across the rocks. I have to admit, she did look wise and clever. It was great sport for the marmots which had been playing this game with coyotes for years. A furry little creature would poke up its head, whistle, wait till the last minute, then pop back into the hole. Thirty seconds later it would appear from another hole and repeat the process. It reminded me of those pop-up prairie dogs that kids try to hit with a plastic bat at the fair. Only once in ten years did Chelsea manage to corner one. She backed a huge angry male marmot into a recess along the riverbank.

It hissed and spat a warning through two large lethal teeth. Neither animal seemed willing to commit to a bloody clash. Chelsea bayed like a bluetick hound until I came up, patted her, and said, "good dog." Then she wagged her tail and trotted off.

I mentioned Chelsea's ability to pick up scents. Since our property borders the woods, this created late-night problems. Deer regularly plunder my wife's flower beds; coyotes traverse our yard in search of the local cats; and bears amble through on nightly forays of the neighborhood garbage cans. Nothing went through our yard without an alert from the dog. She would run from door to door placing her nose at the sill and sucking air like a vacuum cleaner. Then the barking. Then the chase. That was me chasing the dog through the house trying to get her under control. I tried shouting, treats, the spray bottle, everything I'd ever read or imagined. Sometimes she resorted to subterfuge and gave me the "I have to go pee" routine. For that, we had a long tether. Without it, she would jump the fence and take off.

One particular night she gave the "go pee" whine. I was suspicious. Earlier that night we had gone through the barking, sniffing, running through the house drill. I carefully slid open the patio door and reached for the tether. Chelsea bolted out the door and over the fence. BARK, BARK, BARK. My poor neighbors. I was already messed up for the night and looking at a long, tired day on the job. I called and called. "COME, COME, COME!' I whistled. The poor neighbors. The barking gradually faded up the mountainside. *I hope the coyotes get you, you little twit.*

I went back to bed. An hour later, BARK, BARK, BARK. I pulled on my jeans and staggered out the back door. BARK, BARK, BARK. She was at the base of a large Ponderosa pine that separated our house from the neighbor's. Clinging ten feet up the trunk of the tree was the biggest black bear I'd ever seen. "Good girl," I said, at which she stopped barking and gave me that "Look what I did. Aren't you proud of me?"

I pounded on the bedroom window, "Lin, come out here, you've got to see this."

Something I've noticed in scary movies; when a beautiful woman goes outside at night to check on some mysterious sound, she always wears a flimsy transparent nightgown. Well, apart from the fact that Lin wears a thick flannel nightgown that extends from her neck to her ankles, you get the picture. She walked about halfway across the back yard and whispered, "What is it?"

I pointed, "Look!"

Mr. Bear suddenly turned and hissed. Lin appeared to levitate, turn toward the patio door, and evaporate into the house. A ghost couldn't have done better. Chelsea gave me her "You take care of this one and I'll go get another one" tail wag. I grabbed her collar. *I don't think so, you little dimwit. You and I are going in the house.*

When she was about ten, she wasn't her old self. She no longer met me at the door when I came home from work, and she spent most of the time sleeping. If I brought out the shotgun, she would come to life, and she still enjoyed a good walk but not a long run. We were out one day on a trail below our house. Coming up the path, a young girl was leading a large German Shepherd. It jerked the leash from the girl's grip and viciously attacked Chelsea. I have to say, my little dog went into "protect" mode, but was no match for that bruiser. I managed to get them apart without getting bit. The girl was in tears. I told her not to worry, no damage done. Wrong!

When I got home, Chelsea laid down and began licking her lower left side. I noticed she was bleeding and upon a closer look found a tear in her abdomen. Off to the vet we went. I dropped her off and returned home. I had just sat down for coffee and the phone rang. It was the vet.

"I've examined your dog. Before I stitch her up, we need to have a talk. Can you come down to the clinic?"

I arrived and was ushered into an exam room.

The vet stared at the floor and shook his head. "I've bad news. Your dog is full of cancer. See this lump on her neck? She has tumors like this throughout her body. We need to discuss your options."

"Options?"

"I can stitch up her wound and we can start chemo right away."

"Chemo?" I had grown up on a farm and we took good care of our animals but chemotherapy for a dog? Chelsea had reached the average life expectancy for a Springer. Chemo? But she was part of the family.

"What would it cost?"

"We can start for around three thousand dollars."

"Three thousand dollars!?"

"Or I can prescribe prednisone. She'll feel like a puppy for about six weeks and then quickly go downhill. Keep in mind, no matter what you decide, she still needs surgery and about three weeks recovery time unless you choose to have her euthanized."

I believe the most loving thing you can do for an animal if it's suffering is to put it to sleep but I just couldn't let go of a pet that had been my best friend and constant companion for ten years. And what about my wife and kids. Chelsea was part of the family.

I wiped a tear from my left eye, "How much will the prednisone cost?"

"About fourteen dollars."

"I'll get the prednisone and have you stitch the wound. I'm not ready to let her go and my family needs some time to accept losing her."

Three weeks of recovery from the tear in her abdomen seemed like such a waste of the little time we were promised. Chelsea improved quickly. Overnight she was like her younger self. She began jumping the fence and taking off once again, the little twit. It happened to be bird season, so shotgun, dog, and hunter took to the forest. Her final hunt was in the back woods behind the Bachelor area of Kamloops. I parked the truck on an old bush road and ambled up a path through the trees. The object was not to shoot a grouse but rather, to let Chelsea enjoy a final romp in the wilds. Believe it or not, she flushed a covey of a dozen or more grouse, the largest flock I had seen in years. Of course, she was working slightly out of shotgun range so I couldn't get a shot. Remember the first two pheasants she flushed? You can guess what happened. The birds scrambled like a squadron of World War II Spitfires; Chelsea went into pursuit mode; and I was left with an empty game bag looking like the poor victim of a snipe hunt.

"Chelsea," I called. "Come girl. Come!" Silence. I whistled. Almost out of earshot I heard the faint thrumming of wings and a joyful yelp. "Chelsea! Come!" I called until I was hoarse. I whistled until my tongue felt like the dry flap of a worn-out boot. No Chelsea.

Venus appeared on the horizon. One by one, the host of heaven twinkled in the sky. I continued to call and whistle. No Chelsea. Owls hooted back and forth like a party line in old ranch country. *I wonder if they're passing warning messages about a runaway black and white spaniel.* The moon rose in its full glory. Good thing, because I would never have found my way to the truck without its faint illumination. I couldn't bear the thought of facing Lin without the dog. I'm a bit of a skinflint and she would probably think I had shot Chelsea in lieu of paying the vet to put her down. Truth be told, I had thought about it, but my family deserved the chance to say a proper goodbye. With heavy heart and a few tears I stumbled down the darkened trail to the truck. Guess who was lying beside the driver's door with her tongue lolling out and a silly grin. The twit!

Going into the seventh week, Chelsea grew weaker day by day. Every morning my wife and I conferred. *Was this the day?* Finally, I couldn't bear to see her suffer any longer. Lin, Sean, and I took her for one last walk. Can you believe it? She sniffed out a mouse trail and suddenly forgot she was sick. Sniff, sniff, dig, dig, sniff, sniff, dig, dig until coming to a nest. Then the digging began in earnest. We heard intermittent yips of joy, followed by a squeak and a crunch.

Lin looked at me, "Are you sure it's time?"

"There will be no better time."

CHELSEA OBEDIENTLY HEELED when we were led into the vet's exam room.

"Up!" I commanded. She climbed up a stool and crawled onto the table.

"Down." She lay down.

I patted her head. The vet gave her a needle, and for the first time in days I saw the tension and pain ease from her body. She lay her chin on the table and looked up at me with those loving brown eyes one last time as if to say, "Thank you."

Chelsea lies buried on the hillside above our house. A Sunshine Dogwood grows as a memorial of her wonderful companionship. I get more birds without her, but I would gladly trade them all to have her sitting on the passenger seat with her tongue lolling out and her ears flapping in the breeze of an open car window.

What a beauty, great companion, and friend

She looks a bit possessed in this photo. Hmm?

WILD BOARS

WILD PIGS ARE not something you'd expect in British Columbia. I've read and fantasized about hunting razorbacks in the southern swamps of the United States, but this is Canada. Wild boars, really? "Pig" and "problem" both begin with a P, and feral pigs are making their mark. They're oinkers gone wild that originated in Europe and later escaped from local hog farms. When a drift of porkers goes through, it forages, roots, and tramples whatever suits its appetite. Whole crops can be destroyed. Spring calves and lambs are at risk. Water sources are polluted with parasites and diseases like hepatitis. So if you live where pigs roam, best to mind what you drink. And if you shoot one, make certain it's *well done* before biting into a porkchop or a rack of ribs.

The first I heard of local hog hunting was an ad in our community newspaper, "BAG YOUR OWN BACON: Local Farmer Seeks Wild Pig Hunters." I didn't waste time before dialing the number given in the paper.

"You the farmer looking for pig hunters?"

"Why? You wantin' to shoot yourself a hog for the winter?"

"You said it. What's the deal?"

"No deal. Got a drove of swine that need thinnin'. It'll cost you fifty dollars to hunt on my land. If you don't get your hog, you'll get your money back."

Three days later I drove to a small farm about fifty miles northeast of Kamloops. A long dirt track circled around a marshy slough of rushes and cattails to a small log house with a large woodpile neatly stacked along one wall. A barn made from rough-hewn lumber and a rustic chicken coup sat thirty yards behind the house. I looked at a curl of smoke wafting from the chimney and imagined fresh barbecued ribs and a side of cured bacon. I could hardly wait to set my sights on a hairy, black, cob roller.

Knock! Knock! The door opened. "Good mornin'," I said. "I'm the fellow you talked to on the phone."

"Yeah, yeah. Come in. We were just grabbin' coffee and a biscuit. Why don't you join us? Have a seat. I'm Phil Bentley; this here's my wife, Lucille; and that's my twelve-year-old, Marcie. You take cream in your coffee? This is fresh skimmed this mornin'."

The last thing I wanted was to waste time drinking coffee, but it was obvious that Phil didn't get much company and loved to talk. So I fidgeted and squirmed while we discussed the weather, the local hockey team, and livestock prices. I'd never seen a stockyard or cattle auction but as a seasoned hunter, I've mastered the art of the knowing nod and the occasional, "uh huh." We talked about cattle and chickens, the latest pine beetle infestation, and the knuckleheads in government that don't have a clue about ranching. I reckoned the time at the table was part of the cost of shooting a wild boar.

After three cups of coffee and an hour of chin wagging Phil rested his mug on the table and leaned back.

"I guess ya'll be wantin' to get that porker. I'll take the fifty now, though like I said, ya'll get it back if ya don't take home a hog. Marcie will be ya're guide and help ya pick one out."

No offense, but I very nearly backed out of the deal. I'd been hunting for nearly forty years and never taken orders from a twelve-year-old. If Marcie could just show me which direction to hunt, I'd be obliged. No such luck. So I left the house, went to my truck, and shouldered my .308 Browning. Then I walked to the woodpile where Marcie stood waiting.

"This way, sir," she said. We hiked behind the house and stopped at the barn. She opened the door. "Follow me."

Twelve pigsties lined one side of the building. Marcie pointed to each pig as we walked down the center aisle. "That's Waddles. Daddy says we'll only keep her till next spring. She used to have two or three litters a year. That's almost thirty piggies. But she's getting old now. This is Olivia. She's my pet." Marcie gave me the stats and history of Wilbur, Squealer, Daisy, Huxley, Pinky, and Porky. She stopped outside the sty of a monstrous razorback. It had black, spikey hair, and long angled tusks. "That's Hogzilla," she said.

He's getting mean and has run off a couple times. Daddy says he'll make a bacon bonanza for some lucky hunter." The boar's dark, dull, menacing eyes met mine. Marcie continued, "Daddy says that you're welcome to shoot any of the boors except Wilbur. He's our breeder."

I was nonplussed. This was not the hunt I had expected. I sized up Hogzilla. He weighed at least four hundred pounds and would dress out around two hundred fifty. That's only twenty cents per pound. But what would I do with that much pork, and probably pretty tough and stringy too? Then I looked at Huxley. I imagined him on a spit in the backyard with the neighbors cutting off slices of succulent leg and loin. Yep. Huxley was the porker for me.

Most of my neighbors are hobby farmers. There's the chiropractor, the computer programmer, the truck driver, the teacher, and a half dozen retirees. Rancher wannabes usually settle for a couple acres, a small barn, and a fashionable horse. Few "hobby" horses ever get ridden, but they add status. Just expensive lawn ornaments if you ask me. We all get along and everyone enjoys a backyard barbecue. Fifteen friendly neighbors gathered in my yard to share a "wild" boar that was roasting on an open spit. Chips, potato salad, baked beans, and corn on the cob were laid out buffet-style on a long table. Rhubarb, apple, and cherry pies awaited in the kitchen. A couple teenagers cranked away at an old-fashioned ice cream maker. This was a BYOB (Bring Your Own Booze) occasion to which guests never disappointed and willingly shared. A few people enjoyed the hot tub. A competitive group of men gathered at the horseshoe pit. Wives shared the latest neighborhood gossip. The hunting group gathered round me at the fire.

Harvey Williams sipped from a Corona. "Tell us how you got your boar," he said.

"Yea," added Melvin Forbes. "What's it like hunting for a wild pig?"

I squinted from face to face of the small crowd. "Well," I said. "I've hunted grizzlies; I've faced down black bears; and I've been tracked by cougars. I've been struck at by a rattle snake, and I've shot copperheads. But the closest I ever come to being torn to pieces was by that sounder charging through the marsh grass." The fellows fell silent as I gave a "knowing" nod. "The ranch where I was hunting has a large marshy bog that stretches across an immense swath of semi-wilderness. I'd been following a cow path around the edges where the reeds and cattails blend into the trees when I came across tracks from a drift of pigs. I soon came to a muddy spot where they'd been digging. Half-eaten roots littered the ground. Holes appeared where they'd nosed under rotten logs and dead trees. They'd had a real feed fest. Had to watch my step getting around all the pig poo. They can do an extraordinary amount of damage. It's no wonder farmers and ranchers hate the nasty critters."

I shook my head and grimaced before continuing.

"All was quiet and still when suddenly there was movement in the swamp grass. I don't mean a small flutter here and there. There was a mass parting of the grass, accompanied by wild grunts and squeals coming right at me. A savage boar burst through the reeds not ten feet away. I only had time to raise my rifle waist high and fire. Smacked him right between the eyes."

During the silence that followed I tried to gauge each man's thoughts. Hunters have great imaginations.

Harvey broke the silence. "No way! That's the biggest pile of bull I ever heard!"

"Way!" I replied. "Do you think I'd lie to my nearest neighbor? Look at that porker. There's the bullet hole right between its eyes."

Melvin stared into the flames where fat dripped and sizzled on the coals. In a low voice so his wife at the nearby buffet table wouldn't hear, he said, "What are the chances of lining up a hunt for us?"

I DROVE TO the Bentleys and again sat for coffee and a chitchat.

"Phil," I said. "I want to give some fellas a hunt they'll never forget. I'll collect the money for ya and there's no need for refunds. They'll get their money's worth whether they shoot a porker or not."

Turning to Marcie, I continued. "Marcie, I'll need your help. Instead of bringing the guys to the pigsties, I need you to shoo those oinkers out the back of the barn and into the marsh. That'll give the pigs a sporting chance. In the meantime I'll drop the men off in the tall grass and willows on the other side of the bog.

"Phil, is there some way to scare those porkers into a run through the marsh?"

Phil had the biggest grin you can imagine. "No problem," he said. "Me and Bruiser, that's my dog, will have those hogs running like greased pigs at a summer picnic."

BACK IN KAMLOOPS my buddies could hardly contain themselves. You'd have thought we were going on safari in Africa. Whereas I usually hunt in an old jacket and blue jeans, my city "hunters" could have made a fashion statement for Cabela's with their new camo jackets and trousers. Clothing may make the man, but it doesn't do much for the hunter. Typical of men, this was an excuse for new knives and premium ammunition. After all, the meat would more than pay for any expense. *Really?* Harvey bought himself a .300 Weatherby Magnum. Made me wonder if he knew the difference between a three-hundred-pound boar and a fifteen-hundred-pound bison.

The boys and I arrived at the Bentley's on a crisp Saturday morning. No one had slept much the night before, their pre-hunting dreams filled with spikey haired sows and ivory tusked boars. Harvey Williams and Melvin Forbes, along with Fred Steele and Norm McLeod, clamored out of my derelict Bronco at the far end of the marsh.

"You fellows wait twenty minutes and then begin working your way through the bog," I said. "Phil Bentley will meet me at the other end, and we'll drive those oinkers right to ya. He'll be happy to be rid of the foul things." As I drove away, I glanced in the rearview mirror. The guys were loading their rifles and checking their gear. I had a good chuckle. *Those new boots and nice outfits will soon ooze mud and muck.*

Phil invited me in for coffee while Marcie went to the barn to sort the pigs. I wanted to draw the experience out, so I took my time enjoying a good brew and a fresh baked cinnamon bun. No point in going to all this trouble without giving the guys a good workout. We finally sauntered out to the pigsties where Marcie had assembled a small drift of pigs. As soon as she opened the rear gate of the barn those cob rollers charged into the swamp grass. It reminded me of jailbirds escaping from the big house. You never heard so much oinking, squealing, and grunting as they fled into the weeds. Phil and I, along with Marcie and Bruiser, followed to ensure the animals ploughed into four unseasoned "wild boar" hunters. Within minutes the shooting began. Words like @$&% and $!*&% peppered the air. I thought I heard someone holler, "RUN!" Soon, the porkers were streaming past us headed back toward the barn. I laughed so hard I nearly wet myself.

My sidesplitting stopped when the upper tips of the tall swamp grass snaked toward me and suddenly stopped about ten feet away. The grass parted and a large snout protruded followed by dark beady eyes set above two razor-sharp tusks. *Hogzilla!* I hightailed it for higher ground and frantically shinnied up a birch sapling. The boar, which had been on my heels, settled at the base of the tree. It seemed to know I would have to come down sooner or later. Then the spindly little tree began to bend and arch under my weight. I was soon nearly upside down and only five feet from the waiting Hogzilla; then four; then three. Warm liquid pooled in my blue jeans and began to dribble up my belly as Hogzilla's snout snorted only two feet below my nose. He smacked his lips and grunted. *God, if you just get me out of this one, I promise...* Bruiser hurdled from the brush. I was saved.

Phil Bentley saw the whole thing. He told me he wished he'd had a camera. There had been a lot of shooting, but every pig returned to the barn unscathed. Phil offered a refund. I assured him that I hadn't mentioned refunds to my buddies. So long as he kept my encounter with Hogzilla our little secret, he was welcome to keep the two hundred dollars. As for Harvey, Melvin, Fred, and Norm, I drove them to Phil's farmhouse where they each paid another fifty dollars for a *domestic* pig. The four then confabulated a story for their wives and swore me to secrecy. As for Hogzilla, Phill decided the old hog had proved his merit and decided to keep him for another year.

THE BASS MASTER

LIN AND I occasionally drive along the Oregon coast when visiting our American relatives. Every time we drive through Depoe Bay I'm reminded of the wind, rain, and upchuck of my first fishing trip on the ocean but my love of fishing is greater than my fear of nausea. Eventually I talked my wife into a morning of charter fishing. I explained that the fish we caught would easily cover the cost of licenses, equipment, and the guide. That's a ploy fishermen and hunters have used from the time a cave man negotiated with his woman for trading their warm bear hide for a new stone pointed spear. "With new spear, me get not one, but two bear, maybe more." Archeologists occasionally dig up a Neandertal that froze from exposure, spear in hand. We booked from the same dock in Depoe Bay as my first ill-fated experience. The weather was sunny, but I knew from experience that the Pacific Ocean is cold, especially with a little wind and chop. We stopped at a thrift store and bought a couple cheap, ratty-looking winter coats and hats. Warmth far surpasses fashion on the frigid waters of the Pacific. Next, we shopped at a pharmacy for the most potent motion sickness medication available. The druggist recommended Dramamine.

The following morning I took a double dose on the way to the pier. Lin has misgivings about medications and choked down half a tablet. By 5:30 we had purchased our licenses and were carefully descending the slippery steps that wind to the pier. A Frenchman named Pierre welcomed us and a half dozen other fisherman wannabes aboard the *Phantasma.* Just as Pierre was loosing the mooring lines, four young people came rushing down the stairs. "Wait!" shouted a young woman in her mid-twenties. "Wait. My grandpa is coming!"

An elderly man slowly inched his way down the steps. It was his seventy-ninth birthday and the grandchildren had made a last-minute decision to take him ocean fishing, something he had always wanted to do. And something they may have done in the Caribbean but obviously had never done in the North Pacific. The group clambered aboard wearing summer flipflops, shorts, and tank tops – well dressed for the beach. Pierre rolled his eyes and grimaced as he helped them one by one onto the deck. I nudged Lin and shook my head.

The captain of the vessel, Jim Parsons, idled the *Phantasma* under a highway bridge and then hit the throttle. There's something exhilarating about crashing through the breakwater to the open ocean. Soon the craft maneuvered through swells and dips.

Up, up, up. Down, down, down. About twenty minutes out Captain Parsons idled the craft to a stop so folks could lower the crab pots which were an option of our excursion. Then we were off to the open sea. At thirty minutes out three of the birthday party were huddled in the cabin trying to keep warm and occasionally rushing on deck to vomit over the side, and a middle-aged woman was laid out on the galley table where she remained motionless for the next four hours. Grandpa, bless his heart, was seated on a corner of the stern opposite Lin. He didn't feel a thing. I suspect he was on medication. Pierre had given him a fleece-lined rain slicker and stocking hat.

Among the other passengers were two Basque brothers, Ander and Anton, who were treating their dad to a trip. They were dressed warmly, but clearly came from a city where fashion was important. Their father, Deunoro, was a shepherd from Idaho, a real down to earth guy with a great sense of humor. The sons must have taken after their mother. They were dour and quiet.

Captain Parsons sailed to a known fishing ground and idled the *Phantasma*. "Lines out!" shouted Pierre. We quickly lowered our lines to the sea bottom and then reeled up about a foot as we had been previously instructed. The wave action gently jigged the lures up and down.

"Fish on!" cried Lin as she reeled in a massive sea bass.

Got to love that gal. I've never seen anyone enjoy bringing in a fish like she does. This turned out to be a challenging outing. With all the upchucking going on around her, she soon began heaving over her own corner of the starboard every hour or so. Unlike those poor, cold, landlubbers huddled in the cabin, Lin's love of fishing kept her at the rail. She cried "fish on" more than anyone else. I accused her of attracting bass to her corner by chumming, a practice of attracting fish by throwing bait into the water. You wouldn't believe all the "bait" floating around her line. She soon had her limit and began filling the fish tubs of the Basque brothers. Pierre made her his favorite and gave her the title of "Bass Master."

I was having a great time. The double dose of Dramamine made me higher than a cat on a telephone wire. I felt like a seasoned seaman.

One of the Basque boys, Anton, jigged a fish. He whispered, "fish on," and had a citified way of reeling as though he was afraid he might get his hands dirty. I gave him an incredulous look, "What did you say?" Poor guy looked embarrassed.

"Fish on," he mumbled.

"What?" I exclaimed. "Ya got to say it like ya mean it. And don't worry about breaking that darned reel. Bring that sucker up before it gets away." He gave me a scared look and stopped reeling. "Come on," I blurted. "Ya here to fish or just enjoy the scenery?" I waved at Pierre who was helping a young novice at the bow. "Fish on!" I screamed. "Fish on! This fella's got a fish!"

I turned back to Anton. "Ya got to get the man's attention if ya want any help. Ya stick close to me, and I'll learn ya how to fish."

They say there's some good in everyone. Anton was well dressed and wasn't bad looking for a guy, but he sure didn't know how to fish; and he's not someone I would invite to a party.

With Lin's help everyone had their limit and Captain Parsons set sail for shore. Even though I hadn't signed up for crabbing, I helped pull the pots. Those poor people laid out in the cabin would have fish and crab to show for their misery, but I doubt that they showed any slides or home movies of their grandpa's birthday trip. Speaking of which, he was the only person in the family that didn't get sick. He and Deunoro hit it right off. Both had grown up in the 30s and both knew how to yell, "fish on!" Or in Deunoro's case, "arrain on!" That wasn't English or French, but Pierre knew what he meant.

The *Phantasma* chugged into its protected bay, an instant cure for seasickness. We clambered onto the dock. A few, who looked pale and sickly, staggered behind. Several locals met us with a gargantuan boiling pot for the crabs and a filleting table for the bass. As the *Phantasma* idled from the dock to refuel, Pierre waved and tipped his hat.

Lin and I loaded our catch in the car, deposited our coats and hats in a dumpster, and drove to a local supermarket to pick up freezer bags and a small Styrofoam cooler. We pulled into a city park and bagged fifteen pounds of fillets, not bad for a morning of fun and camaraderie. Then I returned to the car and settled back for a ten-minute nap. Two hours later I came to. Dramamine sure knocks ya out. I had the driest mouth you can imagine, a second side effect of the drug. If I went fishing every day like that I'd probably turn into a giant raisin.

WHEN I RETIRED, my sons, Mike and Sean, changed my fishing excursions forever. They had deliberated between a one-week fishing trip of a lifetime versus a lifetime of fishing with a boat. They decided that the incremental enjoyment of a small boat outweighed the short-term delight of a fishing lodge. The boys went to work reconditioning a twelve-foot aluminum boat and overhauling a 1970s Honda 7.5 HP outboard. It was truly a work of love. With both sons and all the grandsons in on the project it's a miracle that no one spilled the beans. What a surprise when Mike pulled a boat with motor and fully licensed trailer in front of our home in Kamloops. I soon christened the craft as the *Seagull.*

Prior to that I had gone salmon fishing on the South Thompson River for Chinook with a friend who taught me how to troll, but not having my own boat was a hindrance. I'd tried every trick I knew fishing from shore: lures like Dodgers and FSTs; large spinners of every size, shape, and color; and enough salmon roe to start a hatchery. I could start a sporting goods store with all the gear I lost on the bottom of the river. In probably a hundred hours spread over three years I caught one Chinook. That changed somewhat with the boat. If I put in the time, I'd catch the odd salmon but hardly enough to justify hours of putt-putt-putting up and down the river, days of cold fingers and wet clothing, and the expense of gas and oil. I had yet to discover a formula that works for me.

There are two basic techniques for catching fish. One is trolling and the other is plunking. The second is done either from shore or from an anchored boat. It simply means that you "plunk" the lure or bait into the water and let the fish come to you. I've seen it done with spinners, with salmon roe, and with plugs. It wasn't until the Bass Master joined me that I changed my method. For me, fishing had become akin to doing penance, meaning that the reason for being there was to suffer. Catching the odd fish was a side benefit. Lin isn't much for suffering. She was quick to notice that boats that anchored midstream were catching fish. They were also secured where people could visit back and forth, enjoy a good picnic lunch, and even take a nap. Let the fish do the work. After three long fruitless days trolling up and down the river without a hit, Lin felt that we had disgraced our boat, our children, and several generations of my First Nations ancestors.

She was determined to catch a salmon and insisted that we anchor among the "plunking" crowd on our next trip. I didn't realize how much I had been missing. The other fishermen were willing to share bait, advice, and even minor tackle. I soon learned that I hadn't been properly baiting roe for the past five years. No wonder I never had any luck. One fellow was having great success with Brad's Cut Plugs. He showed me how to use them but wished me luck in finding a plug or any other salmon gear so late in the season. As soon as we got back to town I scoured the sporting goods stores for spider thread (for securing roe), plugs, tuna fish (bait), and a much larger net. No more "Mr. Nice Guy!"

I was on my own the next time out. The fishing ground was crowded, and I didn't want to risk banging into other boats, so I anchored upstream about fifty yards from the main group. I dropped a Brad's Cut Plug to the bottom and *wham*, I had a salmon. I landed only one that day, but I'd found the right spot to bring Lin. I could hardly wait. When we arrived at 7:00 am the following Saturday, Lin had a salmon within the first twenty minutes. Half an hour later she had her second. Then I landed one. Another boat soon anchored alongside. We watched a ten-year-old pull in his first Chinook. As he dropped his Dodger back into the water a second salmon struck before he could let out his line. Soon his dad caught the biggest fish he had ever landed. We weren't in the seventh heaven, but we had definitely arrived in the sixth.

That was my best fishing year ever. The Bass Master has now earned a second title, "The Salmon Queen." She loves catching fish. We ended the season early when I convinced her that we needed to leave room in the freezer for venison.

I STILL ENJOY fishing from the bank, and there is nothing more enjoyable than joining a clutch of old codgers during a run of pink salmon. George, a buddy of mine at the Toyota dealership, introduced me to the art of flossing. That's a method of fishing in which a round 1½ to 2-ounce weight called a Bouncing Betty[6] is attached to a leader approximately the same length as your pole. At the end of the leader a piece of yarn or other fluff is secured to the hook. This is launched as far as possible into the middle of the river. The weight "bounces" along the bottom while the leader snakes and whips through the current. When the pinks are running, the line is drawn across the open mouth of a nice fish and snags it, thus the term "flossing." Anglers space themselves along the bank. The person furthest downstream casts first, followed by the next in line, and so forth. If every angler follows the pattern, the fishing lines run parallel, and everyone is happy. When a salmon strikes, you shout, "fish on," and other anglers reel in to avoid tangling the lines. The salmon is pulled to shore, drug onto the beach, and immediately dispatched before it can squirm and shimmy back to the water. When a novice, not mentioning any names, casts out of order or doesn't reel in and gets tangled in a neighbor's line, some fellows get a little hot under the collar. On the third or fourth infraction words may be exchanged. After multiple offenses he may find himself alone on an

---

[6] The name, Bouncing Betty, originates with the S-mine developed by Germany during World War II. The Allied infantry called it a Bouncing Betty because of the psychological effect of a weapon intended to maim rather than to kill. Soldiers had to "watch their step."

outcrop where he couldn't catch a salmon if his life depended on it. Don't ask me how I know. However, I carry several different jackets and hats so I can slip back into line when I feel I've done sufficient penance. During the season, George raced from the sales office every night to floss pinks. He'd be casting from a pebbled beach even if there were only a few minutes left till dark. Salmon after salmon was caught and released because he didn't care for fish; he just liked catching them. He was plain fool crazy about catching fish. I have a couple issues about his style. First, I'm not convinced that a salmon that's played out is still fit to fight the current to the spawning ground. Second, guys like George are keeping other fisherman from stepping into what is obviously a sweet spot. However, I listened intently as George explained how to rig rod and line.

The following Sunday I left early in the morning for a rocky beach near Savona, British Columbia. A dozen men and a couple ladies were lined up along the bank when I arrived. Fellows were fishing and swapping yarns. A few were taking a break and enjoying coffee and sandwiches. I saw a guy hook a fish and then transfer the pole to his crippled buddy. The unspoken rule is that you can help a friend, but he has to bring the fish to shore. In many respects flossing for pinks reminds me of scout camp. It's great fun.

I pulled into the parking area, strode to the beach, and assembled my favorite pole. It was two feet shorter than any other rod in use and not designed for bottom bouncing, but you make do with what you have. I followed George's instructions the best I could remember. I clipped a 1½ ounce weight to the end of my line and attached eight feet of leader. This made casting with a six-foot rod a challenge. George had insisted that the more leader the better. Not having a total grasp of tackle and technique, I tipped the leader with my largest trout fly. Then I squeezed between two anglers and with my first cast immediately snagged my neighbor's line. He glared at me and scrutinized my gear.

"You call yourself a fisherman?" he said in a thick Quebec accent. "You think the fish, he is blind? You never catch a fish with yellow line!"

I was chagrined, but I wanted to catch a salmon. I dug into my tackle box and found a roll of clear leader to replace the yellow. Ten minutes later I tried my second cast, then my third, then...and then.

Frenchy shouted, "Fish on!" and played a nice pink onto the beach. He then stepped beside me as I reeled in my line, reached over, and grabbed the leader. "Let me look," he said. A wooly bugger designed for catching trout dangled from his large, sunburned hand. "You think the fish, he swim all the way from the ocean for this? You never catch a fish with this! I show you how to catch the fish." He showed me a hook with a small piece of red yarn attached. "That what you need to catch the fish." I tell you what, *Anglais,* I give you fish." With that, he looked into his cooler and pulled out the smallest pink salmon I've ever seen, but I was grateful. I don't like facing my wife with an empty creel at the end of a day of avoiding household chores. Remember my grouchy grandpa? He'd leave the house in the morning with his pole and tackle, spend the day playing poker with his buddies, then stop by the supermarket to pick up a couple fresh fish on his way home. He was a crafty old bugger. There's a bit of him in my makeup, though I don't think of myself as "grouchy."

I soon outstayed my welcome in the lineup and moved downstream where I could fish without getting in people's way. It was a terrible spot. I snagged a hidden log or stump so many times that I ran out of hooks, but I mastered my fishing knots. Being too proud to beg gear from the anglers upstream, I sauntered up the beach looking for hooks and weights lost by beginners like myself. You can usually find all the gear you need if it's a popular spot. Yarn and fluff often blow out of some careless angler's tackle box. Hooks and weights are harder to find. I followed a strand of old line to where it wrapped around a small boulder. Lo and behold! A weight and hook. The weight was beat up from multiple bottom bouncing; the hook was rusty; and the fluff was sun-bleached and tacky. Well, beggars can't be choosers. It was my first chance for a close look at what other fishermen were using. I studied it carefully before transferring the weight and hook to my line. Third cast, "fish on!" I soon lost the hook and reluctantly drove home. Next time out I wore a different hat and jacket and slipped back into the lineup. By the end of the season I had six fine pinks in the freezer.

ICE JIGGERS

WHY SUFFER WINTER when you can embrace it? I mean, this is Canada, eh? Winters are much shorter if you wax up the cross-country skis or strap on a pair of snowshoes. The mountains were created for Alpine skiing. For those who can't afford the above, I recommend ice fishing. I love to talk about the time I brought home three hundred pounds. Listeners are dumbfounded.

"Really?"

"What kind?"

"How'd you do it?"

"Where were you fishing?"

I shake my head and answer, "Ya know, that's a lot of ice to get into the trunk of the car."

It's taken me years to warm up to ice fishing. Unless you have a fishing tent, ice fishing is generally left to old crackpots like myself; crazies who enjoy freezing their buns while jawing for several hours on what the government should be doing or why the folks on the other side of the border are to blame for all the world's problems. These conversations are tempered by which side of the border you happen to be fishing. I can't say ice fishing is good exercise, though you do lift your arm several times an hour to wiggle your jig.

My first experience was in Northwestern Ontario. A group of church friends convinced me that I couldn't call myself a real fisherman until I pulled a perch or some other unwary marine creature through the ice. The challenge to my "fisher-manhood" had to be answered. They offered to supply all the tackle and pack the food. The guys must have thought that having a "holy man" along would guarantee a successful day.

We clamored into two cars and drove about ten miles out of Thunder Bay to one of the dozens of lakes surrounding the community. A couple fellows began gathering wood and preparing a fire while the others took me about ten yards out on the ice. I had never seen an ice auger before and watched intently as a Finnish fellow named Vilho began drilling the first of four holes needed for our group.

"You want to give it a go?" He said.

"Sure."

Guys generally have the opinion that a pastor has never done any "real" work. Oh, they appreciate a good sermon and see the need for a man of the cloth to expedite the departure of old folks to heaven, but deep down they suspect that fellows who couldn't operate a chainsaw or pound a nail opted for the ministry. They'll test your physical prowess every chance they get. I started working the handle as a very dull blade began shaving a hole through the ice. By six inches I was sweating, and my flabby biceps were complaining.

"Pastor, you want me to take over?"

"No, I'm fine." *I'm not going to let you guys think I'm a pansy.*

After one foot of cranking I could barely move my arms. I recalled a fellow I'd read about that had burst an aneurism while ice fishing. The obituary said that he was found lying on the ice, "his auger by his side."

"You sure you don't want me to drill for a while? The ice is almost two feet deep."

"No, no. I'm just getting warmed up." *Two feet? I wonder what they'll write in my obituary.* The auger finally chipped through the final inch of ice. *I've been saved!* I passed the auger to Vilho.

"Vilho," I said. "I need to talk to Charlie. It may take a while. Do you mind if I leave the rest to you?"

I retreated to the fire where Charlie was poking through an old tackle box.

"So Charlie," I said. What do I need to know?"

"Nothing to it," he replied. "You're going to love this. Go over there and cut yourself a short willow branch. Don't take off the tip. I'll rig up a line and meet you on the ice."

Vilho was sweating through the third hole when we arrived. Charlie tied the line to the tip of the branch and pulled a plastic bag from an inside coat pocket.

"These are maggots," he explained. "You keep them inside your coat so they won't freeze." I perceived a sly wink to Vilho as he continued. "Some fellows throw a handful in their mouth. That keeps them warm and makes it easier to find one when you rebait your hook, that is, if you can keep them in your cheek. They're quick little devils. Here's how you put one on your hook." *Thank you, Charlie. How can you stand to touch one of those things?* "I always put two or three on at a time. You can do the other two for practice." *Ugg! You can do this, Terry. You'll never live it down if you don't. Show no fear. Ugg!*

Charlie grinned at Vilho and watched as I gingerly mangled two little maggots onto the hook. "Looks like you've done this before." *Not on your life.* "Now we just drop the line in the water and poke the heavy end of the branch into the snow. When the tip jerks, you've got your fish. You don't even have to stand out here. Let's get back to the fire."

The guys had packed a ring of garlic sausage, several bags of chips, and a sixpack of Moosehead Lager. Standing beside a warm fire with a bottle of beer in one hand and roasting a two-inch slice of sausage with the other is a great way to enjoy an afternoon of ice fishing. Let the pole and line do the work while you chew the fat beside a warm fire. I glanced toward our makeshift poles; one, two, three... *What's this? Where's my pole?* I ran onto the ice. Hook, line, and pole, all gone! *Lesson to self: never leave your pole unsecured.*

THE NEXT TIME my feet trod the ice was north of Prince Albert, Saskatchewan. A couple eccentric old brothers, Grygor and Dmitri, coaxed me into a trip. They lived in a weathered old shack on a quarter of rocky land twenty miles northwest of the city. I recall relaxing in their outhouse with the door wide open as I appreciated a spectacular view of the South

Saskatchewan River. My sense of wellbeing was shattered when I pulled up my slacks. The boards didn't meet properly below the seat, and I had just saturated my pants in pee.

Grygor and Dmitri were a funny pair. Dmitri couldn't play or sing a note, but he continually bought expensive violins, exchanging one after another every couple months. He'd proudly show me his latest acquisition every time I was in the area. I guess he thought that eventually he would purchase an instrument that would miraculously change him into a musician. You meet some strange but loveable people in the North.

They showed me how to icefish with live minnows. I felt a pang of compassion for the little fish as I ran a hook through their tails and dropped them into the water. I consoled myself with the thought that since it was ten degrees below zero above the ice and two or three degrees above zero below the ice, they were probably happy to be swimming around in the "warm" water, at least until a pike or pickerel swam by looking for lunch. We caught a couple pickerel. However, sitting on an open lake with the wind gusting by in minus ten-degree weather isn't an enjoyable way to spend an afternoon.

FURTHER NORTH I met a fellow that lived beside Delaronde Lake. Gordon ran a trapline in the winter and a commercial fishing operation in the summer. He invited my wife and me and two other couples for a day of ice fishing and a fish fry. I expressed reluctance, but he promised that we wouldn't regret the trip. We arrived midmorning and Gordon loaded our group into a 1967 Bombardier Snowcat. The back half sat on rubberized tracks similar to what you'd expect to see on a miniaturized army tank. Large skis protruded from the front for steering. Four portholes lined each side of the cargo/passenger cabin where we sat on benches facing each other. I imagined myself in a Finnish army platoon scooting across the ice along the border with the Soviet Union. After a thirty-minute ride over hummocks of snow and rough icy ridges we arrived at Gordon's fishing hut.

Gordon was a realist and had anticipated that our group would not catch enough fish for a feed. He had driven up the day before and set a net under the ice. That's right, *under* the ice. I find anything to do with fishing interesting and this was entirely new to me. A large hole is chopped through the ice and a device called an ice jigger is used to pull a rope under the ice. First Nations people invented it around 1900. A line is attached to a slotted wooden board that floats against the bottom surface of the ice.[7] When pulled, the line activates a lever that pushes the device away from the hole. If the ice is clear, the fisherman locates the jigger and chops a second hole at whatever distance he chooses. If the ice is cloudy, a second person follows the clicking sound of the jigger to determine where to chop through the ice. The rope is then attached to a net which is pulled beneath the ice from one hole to the other. Ingenious, if you ask me.

---

7 The ice jigger reminds me of a scuba diver I met who dives under the ice. His group take off their ballast and then walk upside down on the underside. You have to love people of the North.

As Gordon retrieved the net I collected the fish. Not my style of fishing but tons of fun. We had a collection of white fish, the odd pickerel, and a half dozen or so burbot. Anything not edible was set aside to be sold to a local mink farm. A guy can learn a lot from folks in the business. We set to filleting fish while our wives stoked the woodstove and greased the skillets. Coming out of the cold and into a warm cabin for hot coffee and fresh fried fillets almost makes me want to start a new religion with a basic fishing theology – "Follow me and I will make you fishers of *fish!*"

MY OLDEST FRIEND, Will, lives in Salmon Arm. He phoned me a couple times a year B.G. (Before Grandkids). Conversations went something like this:

"Hey Terry. You been ice fishing yet?"

"No, but I've been thinking about it." *Not really but I don't want to hurt your feelings.*

"What say we meet at Joyce Lake? The fellas are having good luck there."

"Sounds good to me."

"We'll meet around 2:00. That will give us time for a good talk."

"I've got a few errands to do and won't be there until 3:00 or 3:30."

Truth be told, I like yakking, but I don't hanker to the cold. The fish don't start biting until 4:30 and my retiree buttocks can't take three or four hours sitting on the ice. Will and I don't see each other often. I enjoy a chance to catch up on family news and he's about the only person I can talk to about politics and religion without getting into a fight. After an afternoon on the ice we stop at a café in Falkland for beer and a burger. Then he heads for Salmon Arm, and I drive back to Kamloops.

I've come a long way since our last meeting. I even go by myself if it's a nice day. What changed? An extra set of long johns, waterproof boots with thermal linings, and actual ice fishing equipment. Oh! Did I happen to mention hand and foot warmers? I occasionally even catch a fish.

Ice fishing would be so much easier if the regulations didn't read that you can only "ice fish with one line and one lure, artificial fly or other terminal attractor." It seems to me that the odds of catching anything are slim at best. Making a move and drilling again and again in search for an elusive trout is hard work. Will fudged on this rule one time by drilling an extra hole about three feet from the first. He dropped in a second line with a flasher and baitless hook.

"I'm not actually fishing with that one," he grinned. "Just trying to attract some attention."

It worked. Within five minutes he pulled out a twelve-inch rainbow trout. Funniest thing. The trout flipped, wiggled, and shimmied across the ice and down the second hole; fishing karma for bending the rules.

Having pastored for over twenty-five years, I'm adept at judging the "letter" of the law versus the "spirit." The regulations explicitly state that it's unlawful to "use more than one fishing line, EXCEPT a person who is alone in a boat on a lake may angle with two lines." My next time ice fishing, I brought my inflatable dinghy, loaded it with my gear, and slid it across the ice to a nice weed bed. I drilled a hole through the ice at both ends of the boat, dropped in two lines, and smugly settled back with a hot thermos of coffee. Where's there's a will, there's a way.

"What do you think you're doing?"

Coffee sloshed into my boots as I jolted upright and turned to see a man in government grey with a Conservation patch on the shoulder.

"Uh, uh...hello officer. Nice day isn't it."

"You do know the regulations regarding ice fishing?"

"Yes sir, but I'm fishing 'alone in a boat on a lake' and the law allows me to use two lines." I ruffled through my pack and quickly thumbed through a copy of the regulations. "You see, Sir, it says right here ....“

He shook his head and laughed. I guess you got me this time. Just to show I'm a good sport, I have a little gift in my truck that we're handing out to select anglers on behalf of the Premier. Come with me."

I could hardly contain myself. My first thought was of the salmon flies they had been giving anglers for reporting tagged bull trout. The government's real generous to sportsman who promote conservation. I hopped out of the dinghy and followed him to his vehicle.

As he pulled a large leather wallet from the glove compartment, I asked, "What is it, officer?"

"It's a nice, new ticket for violation of the fish and game laws."

"But officer –“

"– no buts! If you were sitting in the dinghy I might not give you this, but right now you're standing on the shore and have two lines in the water. By the way, do you mind if I use your boat to drag your equipment to my truck. You won't need any fishing gear the rest of this season."

The coffee was congealing into ice in the toe of my left boot as I slogged back to my car. As an expert on "the letter" and "the spirit," I should have known better.

O'HAIR AIR

AS MY DAD entered his 80s, he reached the point that talking about fishing was more fun than packing food, digging worms, fueling the outboard, and making the trip. The same held true of hunting. We'd share our memories, adding deeper layers of fabrication with each telling. Dad loved showing me his guns. He'd only retained three: an old twenty-two which he intended to refinish; a classic Winchester .30-30 that he kept in case he had "one more" hunting trip; and a Ruger .357 Magnum pistol with a faulty trigger mechanism (Dad lived in Oregon). I'd pick up each and take aim at an imaginary deer or a make-believe criminal. A hunter's relationship to his guns is almost as intense as the romance with his wife or girlfriend.

Against my better judgment, Dad applied for a permit to pack his pistol. Understand, at the time he was in his eighties. He rode a mobility scooter whenever he went to town. I tried to imagine him going full speed on his little Scout, firing in the air, and yelling, "Come back here, ya dirty crook! Ya won't get away with my lawn ornament." Or racing down the sidewalk and turning to fire at a pursuer, "Ya'll never take me alive!" I tried to talk him out of it, but he felt a need to protect his wife and home, another typical ploy that gun lovers use to increase their collection. He said he'd just feel better knowing he had it. Thankfully, his application was denied.

I told him that if he planned a hunting trip, I'd be happy to join him, but we never got beyond talking about it. The older I get the better I understand "old" people. I don't like sleeping in a strange bed or on the ground, and I don't like cold weather. If the weather is bad I'd rather be at home in front of the fireplace reading *Field and Stream Magazine*.

Time with Dad got me thinking. Right now I take the grandkids fishing, but the time will come when I'll need them to take me. The same goes for hunting. As long as I can hold my .308 and my cataracts don't get too thick, I'll be able shoot a deer for the freezer. But I'll need help getting it out of the bush. Even now I come close to a heart attack if I have to drag an animal more than twenty or thirty yards.

I failed to bring my sons into the hallowed fraternity of hunters and fishermen, but there's hope for my grandsons, Toby, Tyler, Keegan, and Colton. Without mentioning names, each boy is different. One will eventually model for postcards of the "persistent cuss." Once his mind is set he will not give up. Rain will not deter him. Snow and wind will not stop him. I've been tempted a time or two to buy a fish that I can sneak onto his line. Rain, snow, and ice are hard on grandpas. A second grandson is somewhat similar and a great support for the first. Howbeit, he sometimes accepts the inevitable and moves on to other activities. The third collects equipment, cherishes his gear, and was first to gut and clean his own catch. He insists on learning the whole process from baiting the hook to packing the freezer bags. He loves fishing, but only with a group and only when the fish are biting. The fourth is passionate about casting and reeling, but once he's caught a fish his thought is, *Okay, done that. Now can we have some fun.* With a little cultivation these boys will secure my future on the water.

I was buying the boys little children's poles from the time they could walk. Our first adventure was on the South Thompson River across from the Tk'emlúps Powwow grounds. There's a bend there with a deep hole. Forked sticks protrude from the sand and the occasional strand of broken line litters the rocks. I've never seen anyone fishing there but I have encountered a black bear sitting chest deep in the water swatting at passing salmon while another bruin raided a poor homeless person's tent. After countless trips and hours idled away at that bend I've caught one Dolly Varden which I gave to the fellow whose tent was trashed, one freshwater sculpin, the only one I've ever seen and very rare, and multiple pike minnows. This seemed like the perfect place for the kids to practice casting, digging holes, and throwing rocks. With a little luck we might even catch a fish.

Grandma Lin had packed treats and juice boxes. She brought little shovels, buckets, and cars. Somehow Grandma knows what children need to enjoy an afternoon outing. My job was to rig poles and bait hooks. Since children have short attention spans, I equipped each rod with a little bell, cast the line into the water, and rested it on a forked stick.

"You boys can dig in the sand, run up and down the beach, and explore the shore. We're here for fun. But if you hear a bell ring come running because that means you have a fish."

Papa John, the other grandpa, ambled down the trail to see how we were doing. The boys greeted him with glee as they scampered over sand and rocks. Papa took one look at the fishing rods, rolled his eyes, and shook his head.

"If a fish latches onto one of those," he said, "it will take rod, reel, and all."

I replied, "Not to worry, with all this commotion I doubt there's any fish near here."

At that very moment a rod arched like an arrow into the sky and splashed into the current. I could see it shooting downstream at the bottom of the river. I plunged into the chilly water, missed it on the first try, came up choking and gasping, and dove again. Ta-da! I had it. Grandma and Keegan were running downstream to rescue my hat. Papa John was emptying his pockets and removing his watch preparing to rescue me. Toby and Tyler were cheering. The fish had thrown the hook and was probably behind some sunken boulder having a good fish laugh.

Toby looked at me with admiration. "Do you think it was a salmon, Grandpa?"

"It could have been," I sputtered. "Ya know, it just might have been a big chinook salmon."

As I tried focusing on that little $12.95 rod and reel, it dawned on me that my $500 progressive lenses were missing. Once again Papa John rolled his eyes and shook his head. I love hearing the boys share that story. In their version there is no "could have been" about it. It *was* a salmon for certain. I see the making of fine fishermen in those boys.

No day is complete without a couple fish on the stringer. In the late afternoon the pike minnows began to bite. Digging holes and skipping stones ceased. We were down to business. The boys soon had seven fish of varying sizes. Pike minnows are not game fish and are major predators of salmon fry. Most fisherman toss them in the brush for the bears. Since I hate wasting a good fish, I once tried frying one. Every bite was a mouthful of bones. Now I pickle them. A pickled chunk of pike minnow on a cracker with butter or mayonnaise makes a great treat. I have my pride and up until that day had never, *never,* let other fishermen know that I keep the pike minnows. The grandsons ended that. They marched to the car with their catch dangling from a stringer for all to see.

The boys had yet to catch fish for the frying pan, so I carefully planned a trip to Pinaus Lake south of Falkland, British Columbia. The best time to fish is *anytime* you can escape the city. Still, I follow the fishing charts out of curiosity. We reached the lake on the best day of the month and at the prime time of the day. Pinaus is a wonderful lake for perch fishing, With a limit of twenty per day, children experience the joy of the tug on the rod and the thrill of landing a little fighter *par excellence* for its size. I rented a boat from the Pinaus Lodge, and it was *Anchors aweigh, my boys, anchors aweigh.* In two days we caught close to a hundred little perch. My dream had come true. The grandsons were so hooked on fishing that while I cleaned fish at the fishing station they kept casting from the dock. I began to regret promising that I would keep filleting until there were no more perch in the sink. Each time I reached what I thought was my last fish three more seemed to appear.

Why fillet such a small fish? In my Huckleberry Finn days we cleaned perch whole, cut out the fins, and scaled the little scrappers – a heap of work for a four or five-inch perch. I know from experience that little boys don't like bones, but tiny boneless fillets, floured and fried, taste like heaven when dipped in sweet 'n sour sauce. It was important that the kids not only like catching fish but also enjoy eating their catch.

We've had some great adventures at a remote fishing lodge called The Rustic Resort where we've taken Jana, our daughter-in-law, and the four grandsons to create some fantastic memories. Our favorite lake is Summit. Imagine driving down a narrow road; passing through mountain trees and scrub; edging between huge boulders; and parking at the base of a bald rocky slide. Then you hike across stony bluffs and through scrubby pine. Bear scat litters the occasional bend in the trail. A small garter snake slithers across the path. Finally you step to the bank of an enchanted lake set in the bowl of an ancient volcano

The memory of the three older kids rowing across Summit Lake brings joy to my grandpa heart. Tyler was at the bow; Toby was at the oars; and Keegan was gleefully flicking his pole back and forth at the stern. Grandma Lin, Jana, Colton, and I were anchored within shouting distance. A ruckus soon erupted on the boys' boat. A medium sized trout had flipped off the hook and was circling their craft chomping at the surface like a mini-sea monster. When the fish dove Toby immediately cast his lure into the lake. *Wham! Fish on!* Whether it was the same fish or not is a matter of conjecture, but he had hooked a real fighter. As Toby pulled the trout over the gunnel it twisted loose and nosedived into the murky water. Two seconds later it launched from the water, smacked him in the chest, and dropped into the boat. The boys christened it, O'Hair Air, the Mad Trout of Summit Lake.

Tyler and Toby with their first catch

Keegan shows grandpa how to crab.

Colton at the oars with Caspian the faithful canine

OUR BOAT, the *Seagull,* has opened adventure after adventure. On one occasion the older three boys and I were caught in a thunderstorm while fishing a lake south of Kamloops. We had moored at a crude dock to enjoy peanut butter sandwiches when clouds rolled over the lake, thunder rocked the sky, and the rain fell. A trail through the trees led to an old summer camp consisting of one cabin and a large cook house – everything needed for shelter and a warm fire. When the sun reappeared, it was back to the lake. That day the kids landed the two biggest trout ever to grace the *Seagull.* Toby caught an eighteen inch, 2 ½ pound rainbow trout, a family record. Two hours later, Keegan broke the record with a twenty inch, 3 ½ pounder. In the meantime, Tyler added a couple 1 pounders. It wasn't the most trout we've ever caught but by far the biggest! Shortly after that the battery ran out of power for our electric outboard. I was so grateful to have a muscled grandson man the oars!

AN APPRECIATION OF the outdoors and a "can do" spirit is so important to today's youth. Not long ago Toby phoned me from the bank of the Serpentine River that runs through the city of Surrey. Tyler had just landed a small coho salmon, something that I've never caught. The boys released it, following the regulation that wild coho are not to be retained, but they were exultant. He told me, "Grandpa, if you come for a visit, I'll teach you how to catch one." Now that's the spirit!

Toby, Keegan, and Tyler hold the record for the biggest trout landed in our boat.

THERE'S MORE STORIES to come but today is a New Moon and I need to get to the lake for the prime feeding time.

Other Books by T.D Roth

The Peasant's Gold
The Story of Peter Wing, North America's First Chinese Mayor

As the Windmill Turns
The Memoirs of Wanda Lorene Baker

The Stories of My Father
The coming of Age of Gary Roth

The Seagull
Adventures on Bell Island, NL, 1942

Novelettes Available for Kindle and Kobo Readers

Deceitful
A ghost town named Flyblow

Diablo
The medicine horse from Chamenos

Gone to Texas
Flight, fight, and fright in the aftermath of the American Civil War

About the Author

T.D. Roth grew up in the ranch country of southern Idaho. He has enjoyed a lifetime of adventure in the fields, mountains, lakes, and streams of the Northwestern United States and coast to coast in Canada. He loves a good story and will assure you that these stories must be true. After all, he made them up himself. He's hunted and fished in Idaho, Oregon, and California. After moving to Canada in 1972 his outdoor experience has included British Columbia, Saskatchewan, Ontario, and Newfoundland. He currently lives in Kamloops, British Columbia,

Manufactured by Amazon.ca
Bolton, ON